WHISPERS AND SHOUTS

Embracing the Journey, Enjoying the Dance

Denise Williams

WESTBOW
PRESS®
A DIVISION OF THOMAS NELSON
& ZONDERVAN

WestBow Press
A Division of Thomas Nelson & Zondervan
1663 Liberty Drive
Bloomington, IN 47403
www.westbowpress.com
1 (866) 928-1240

ISBN: 978-1-9736-5712-5 (sc)
ISBN: 978-1-9736-5713-2 (hc)
ISBN: 978-1-9736-5711-8 (e)

Library of Congress Control Number: 2019903181

Print information available on the last page.

WestBow Press rev. date: 04/02/2019

God whispers to us in our pleasures, speaks in our conscience, but shouts in our pain: it is His megaphone to rouse a deaf world.

—C. S. Lewis, *The Problem of Pain*

Contents

Acknowledgments

Few books are written by just one person. Many people walked with me on this writing journey. I want to give special thanks to Kathy Blume, whose pompoms are probably worn out by now. You believed in me and my story before any words were put to paper. Your tenacious friendship has blessed me daily for over twenty years. Without your encouragement, cheering me on when I wanted to abandon ship, editing help, sanity sessions, and willingness to listen to raw material, this book would never have been published. Your enthusiasm and generous spirit amaze me.

Thanks to Betsy Logan for being willing to read rough drafts with a kind yet honest editor's eye. Your critique helped draft the better way to say what you knew was in my heart. Your wisdom was invaluable to the finished product.

To Leah and Maggie, your deep friendships, along with your words of encouragement, tears, and laughter in response to my stories, spurred me on over the years of this project.

Thanks to our small group and the grace group members, who have been vulnerable enough to share your stories and lives with me. You sharpen my ability to see God's redemption in your willingness to stay open and real.

Special thanks to my precious family for your individual expressions of grace over the past few years as I wrote incessantly, lost in the hours. Each of you are the joys of my heart and the inspiration for every page written here. Thank you for the spoken and unspoken encouragement, patience, and belief in me that breathed life into the days my pen sped across the page as well as the days it lay motionless from discouragement. Family is, on all days, a most extravagant gift.

Jordan, your editorial skills were put to good use in helping me say more with fewer words. Your youthful eyes and wisdom made this a much better book.

Norm, you took up the brunt of my slack in my writing absence and became my personal harry-legged cheerleader once again. You are my God-sent man. I love you more each day.

Many thanks to the fine staff at Westbow Press for all their patience and expertise in the editing, design, and publishing processes. Each of you encouraged my first-book efforts with professionalism and grace.

I am forever indebted and grateful to my parents. Mother and Daddy, thank you for your untold sacrifices and belief in me over the years. During each phase of my life, your blood and character has flowed through my veins, and God has used it all to shape me into who I am today. He never wastes a thing. You are both my heroes. I want to be like you when I grow up.

And most of all, thanks to the Holy Trinity, whose eternal dance and giving to one another with no regard to self teaches me how to live. You are my life, joy, light, and hope. You are every breath I take and every word I write. With King David, I sing, "Better is one day in your house than thousands elsewhere." My story is but a grateful drop in the endless sea of Your greater story.

About This Book

This book is a love story within a love story which I've entitled *Whispers and Shouts*. It harkens back to the C.S. Lewis quote which illustrates how God speaks to us more clearly in our pain than at any other moment. Out of His unrelenting love, there are times He turns up the volume in order to rouse the deafness in each of us.

Because God's word is the Christian's plumb line for life and decision-making, I refer to scripture throughout the book. Unless otherwise noted, all references are taken from the New Living Translation (NLT) of the Holy Bible, copyright 1996, 2004.

Introduction

Stories are powerful. My first recollection of their impact came while I sat eating breakfast one morning before getting on the school bus. I listened intently as a deep-voiced gentleman on the radio captivated me with the Kentucky backwoods imagery surrounding a poor, young store clerk named Abraham Lincoln. Like an artist, he painted with bold strokes of how Lincoln had been given six cents too much in a transaction and of his undaunted journey to return the money. The vivid details and character qualities came alive in my young mind, creating images more real than any modern-day flat screen could have displayed. As I looked out the foggy window on my way to school, those still-fresh scenes almost ached to be retold.

After my teacher led our morning pledge to the flag and the prayer for our day, I mustered just enough nerve to walk up to her desk and ask permission to share with the class the story still playing in my head. Taken aback, she looked up from the attendance sheet to confirm my sincerity. Then, as she ushered me to the front of the room, she called for my classmates' attention and set the stage for me to speak.

As I conveyed those images with knees knocking, I remember how it felt to see my friends' eyes widen, eager for each turn of events. Leaning in, they seemed captivated in their seats as I recounted the vivid scenes teeming, eager for an audience. I was amazed to witness how my desire to paint those pictures for them overrode my nerves and strengthened my knees.

Then, after I retook my seat, the teacher quietly left the room.

When she returned, she came straight to my desk, bent down, paid me a nice compliment, and informed me that the other second-grade class would like to hear my story as well. What a resounding encouragement for a seven-year-old, first-time storyteller.

Years later, as a fifth grade teacher, I remember when my own students stilled each other to hear every word and squirmed with excitement as I read. Predictably, each time I approached the last chapter for the day, I heard, "You can't stop there! Just one more, pleeease?" Whether it was to clarify a difficult concept in history, science, math, or grammar, or just for the fun of it, a new air of interest, energy, and eventually hushed silence filled the room when the first words of the story commenced.

Those shared stories created a special bond. They carved out a secret place our classes could retreat to that no one else knew about and very few other students had experienced. Shared bonds, as we all know, are powerful. Those stories also took care of a multitude of potential discipline problems, creating a sense of camaraderie among my students and me. I always loved teaching and made it my trademark to use the element of story as frequently as possible.

The same holds true in the business world. I have seen how powerfully stories translate across cultures and languages in my travels to Paris, Canada, London, and elsewhere for international business trainings. Raucous, half-listening conference rooms filled with thousands come to rapt attention when a speaker begins her story.

Actually, we are all in the midst of a tale of one kind or another; you, me, your eccentric aunt, the postal carrier, the distressed lady at the grocery store, and that mysterious reclusive neighbor. Seeing my own as part of the greater story of the gospel of Christ has forever altered how I see others. And with that new understanding, I never go through an airport or mall, or sit on a park bench without the awareness that each person I pass or sit beside has a story that, if he or she shared it with me over coffee, would change me. As I listen with curiosity, I can't help but marvel at God's sovereign threads of presence and redemption.

Like the multicolored pieces that make up a tapestry, each of our journeys includes joys and sorrows, life and death, peace and turmoil, wounds and healing, loves and losses. And like a grand Weaver, God uses every thread to weave something He alone sees. There are universal needs that impact every story: our insatiable search for purpose and meaning, the desire to know and be known, and our need to love and be loved to name a few.

Even knowing God as the grand Weaver, there have been times in the midst of my darkness when His goodness, mercy, and redemption felt a million miles away. It was in those times when I realized I was looking up at the underside of my tapestry with the messy, gnarled pieces and colors tied off and hanging haphazardly. I have at times mistaken the random underside mess for the top.

By faith and over time, I have come to understand that God works on the other side of the frame, creating a work of beauty I cannot yet see. I am learning to be patient with His process. God tells me He is, even now, making all things new and that we are His masterpieces, created for His glory.

My prayer is that, as you read these portions of my story, God will tune your heart to hear His voice more clearly. I hope you will grasp the vibrant threads of His eternal love for you as well as His amazing grace, sovereign wisdom, and threads of redemption in your own story as you read these parts of mine.

And I also pray that you, along with me, will be able to hear that personal call of the Lion of Judah to "come farther up, come farther in," as C. S. Lewis wrote in *The Last Battle*.

About the Author

The biggest reason I hesitate to share even parts of my story, if truth be known, is because of fear. You see, I am afraid you will have birth-year envy, because I was born in the very best year of all.

1957. Yes, that was the year that produced the "Sweet, Smooth, and Sassy" '57 Chevy Bel Air convertible, yours then for just under $3,000. It was sleek, a baby boomer's dream.

Slinkys were all the rage. Fifty thousand Hula-Hoops per day were being produced in the late 1950s. Elvis, with his velvet-voiced top-twenty hits of "All Shook Up," "Jailhouse Rock," and "Teddy Bear," was a national icon. "Wake up Little Susie," "Tammy," "Bye-Bye Love," and "That'll Be the Day" were jukebox favorites.

An Affair to Remember and *Twelve Angry Men* debuted on the big screen that year. *West Side Story* and *The Music Man* made their premiers on Broadway. *Perry Mason* was launched as a new television drama. *Gunsmoke, The Lone Ranger, Lassie, The Ed Sullivan Show, Leave It to Beaver,* and *I Love Lucy* were some of the shows with the most viewers. And the first version of *Cinderella* was aired, starring a twenty-one-year-old sensation, Julie Andrews.

Was I right? Aren't you just a little envious? Reminiscent at least?

The truth is that I was born at a time when life felt simpler, sweeter, and things happened at a more drinkable pace. I understand the less-than-rosy side to that year and era. But if you're honest, any other year or decade you might pick has its glory side and its downside.

I was, by the grace of God, greatly influenced and shaped by the cultural positives and savory, rhythmic, southern pace of our

North Carolina farming community. I am eternally grateful for hard-working parents and grandparents, who modeled the common-sense values gleaned through everyday life on the farm. It was a rare gift. Almost through osmosis I soaked in respect for people, especially one's elders; honesty; integrity; and attentiveness to the little details that really do matter once you grow up.

As I grew up, I took for granted simple truths that sadly, sound a little old fashioned as I put thought to paper. I have discovered how profoundly important they have proved to be over the decades. Guiding principles like doing a job well and seeing it to the end, saving some of every dollar, looking people in the eye, and respecting the land top the list. We learned the rich value of time and process when it came to raising animals, crops, or children. Life on the farm taught all four of us the value of taking time to observe and revere the way the good Lord made nature.

Common sense was a lot more common then, as were manners and the clear and accepted concepts of right and wrong. The victim mentality had not yet been born. Reverence for God, and respect for country, the rule of law, and those who enforced it was just part of the fabric of our lives. We learned esteem for authority, not out of oppression or blind obedience, but out of an understanding of what lawlessness would bring to our communities and to the country as a whole. That sense of honor and respect lingers in the fiber of my soul today.

Faith, family, and gratitude for our many freedoms were the things that united and defined us as Americans then, even in the midst of the images of chaos we often saw on television. Like baseball and apple pie, our traditions around God, family and country bonded us together and made us proud. And though I can't explain it, we seemed at the same time sincerely humbled and appreciative for all we had been given. Few took those things for granted.

Born just at the end of the Baby Boomer era, that lens is the one through which I write. I hope as you read these stories you will find, no matter what year or era you were born, that they are a little like yours.

chapter 1

Shall We Dance?

He stood tall, lean, and mischievously handsome outside the college classroom where I sat at the front of the room, interpreting for the deaf during that summer school session. My chair was positioned so I could see the deaf students and the professor as well as the goings-on out in the hallway. To my total surprise, his hands moved deliberately as he signed, "Will you go to lunch with me?" in slow but clear sign language.

Though a little amused, I had to admit he had my attention. I recognized him as the roommate of a good friend of mine. He was the cool guy known for his propensity for practical jokes.

I wondered whether he had learned just enough sign language to ask me out. Was he brandishing his idea of fun, or had I just gotten a sincere invitation to lunch? Without missing a beat with my interpreting, I glanced again in his direction. How could I say no to that sincerely expectant, obviously rehearsed smiling effort?

At the Burger Shack a few minutes later, Norm described his dilemma over what we had deemed the best burgers, fries, and shakes in the sleepy little college town of Boiling Springs, North Carolina. He was deep into his final classes before graduating and going to seminary in the fall. His invitation to lunch had come so he could request my help for a few weeks. Being a religion major, Norm had put off this required elementary education class until the shorter summer session. He explained that he really needed to ace this particular class for several reasons. To make that happen, he needed an education major, such as myself, to critique him and give him another set of eyes on his final projects.

Hmmm, a brilliantly devised scheme, I thought.

As a fifth-grade teacher, I was indeed familiar with the kind of children's projects Norm had described. After polishing off my burger, I agreed to his plea for help. Before sliding out of our booth, we set up times the following week to begin work at my nearby apartment.

My routine of walking three miles a day and our mutual love for tennis made it easy for Norm to suggest a little extra time to join me before or after working on his project. Norm's natural athletic abilities, love for playing the guitar, fun-loving nature, enthusiasm for studying God's word, and uncanny ability to make me laugh were some of the qualities that first drew me to sit up and pay attention.

Only a few months earlier, on one of my daily walks, I had made a significant commitment to God to serve Him in whatever field He might call me to. This was a commitment I was prepared to keep, even if it meant I would remain single for the rest of my life. Pictures of the lives of foreign missionaries I had read about flashed through my mind. For two years I had been on an emotional roller coaster from the pain and brokenness of a true love lost. I had finally stopped wrestling and had found a sense of peace. I remember literally holding my hand open in an act of trust as I surrendered my future to God that day.

Because of my previous experience with heartache, a verse I knew well wouldn't leave my mind. "Unless the Lord builds the house, they labor in vain who build it; unless the Lord guards the city, the watchman keeps awake in vain." (Psalm 127:1 NASB) I knew it was true.

So at the ripe old age of twenty-four, I asked God to take over as chief architect of my house and to build it any way He thought best. With that prayer I acknowledged that God alone knew my future. More importantly, it was an admission that I wasn't in control.

In reality, though, instead of real openness to the "any way God thought best" part, I had put up a "No Trespassing" sign on my heart. Parts of it had been safely walled off, closed to any hint of relationship. The pain was much more easily managed and controlled that way.

But the next thing I knew, I found myself looking forward to taking my afternoon walks with a curious newfound friend and making much more frequent use of our community tennis courts. We both seemed to enjoy sitting on the floor of my apartment and playing twenty questions as we designed shadowboxes for theoretical eight-year-olds.

"What do you want to be when you grow up?" I asked while we pasted calico curtains to cardboard, creating a scene from "Goldilocks and the Three Bears."

He told me he wanted to work as a minister of education in a church after he finished his master's degree. His desire was to help people grow in their faith in God and to equip them in sharing it.

I quickly learned that this man contained a depth that went beyond his quiet, fun-loving exterior. Norm was kind, thoughtful, considerate of others, and even serious when he needed to be. To top it all off, the man could dance. With my duties on the farm, studies, and sports involvement, I had never given myself time, opportunity, or permission for such things. But while I was in college, some energetic friends forced me out of my dorm room one night and taught their friend with two reluctant feet to clog. Later that year, my softball buddies made sure this Carolina girl knew how to shag. So at least I had two decent dance moves.

Norm and I discovered our mutual love for beach music, and he taught me some fun, new twists and turns that summer. On top of his confidence on the dance floor, I quickly realized he was one of the few people who could make me laugh aloud at the most unexpected times. Take the time just after we had met that day at the Burger Shack, for example.

I was minding my own business, just walking to my car after a long day of interpreting classes for the deaf. Norm and his roommate, Kelvin, were standing about a stone's throw away on the sidewalk, just outside the campus chapel. They seemed involved in a serious sidebar conversation and barely looked up as I approached. Tired and eager to get back to my apartment and put my feet up, I was a little relieved not to have to make small talk. I waved and smiled briefly before getting into my car. I was looking forward to taking my usual quiet ride home and to unwinding to my oldies station on the radio.

When I started the engine, I'm sure my scream echoed across the campus. Suddenly, the radio belted out some ungodly heavy metal station at the absolute loudest possible volume. The heater blasted onto my already overheated face, and the windshield wipers waved ferociously like someone at a Pentecostal prayer meeting.

Norm and Kelvin congratulated each other as if they had just won the lottery. Then they doubled over in the hilarity and quality of their success. To make matters worse, onlookers approved with a chorus of laughter at my plight. Feeling so proud of themselves, the Bobbsey Twins waved shyly in my direction as they turned and headed for class.

My pursed lips and piercing stare in their direction didn't make a dent in their fun at my heart's expense. I had been played. That fact should have been my first clue. These were silly boys. And they felt no shame at having nearly sent an unsuspecting passerby into cardiac arrest.

But I had to admit that after a few weeks, I was taking notes and paying attention. That was because in my teenage years my pastor had challenged me to brainstorm and make a prayerful list of all the qualities I wanted in a future husband if and when I ever got married. My list was long and quite specific. Anyone in his or her right mind would have thought it impossible for any one man to possess all those qualities. But I trusted that God had meant it when He said, "Take delight in the Lord, and he will give you your heart's desires. Commit everything you do to the Lord. Trust him, and he will help you" (Psalm 37:4–5). My job was to take delight in the Lord. I figured it was God's job to change my heart if my desires were off the mark.

As a starry-eyed teenager, I had read that list over and over and confidently prayed that such a man might really exist somewhere out there. I had been asked to be honest on paper, and so I had. Tucking it away in my nightstand drawer, I had decided that I wouldn't worry or try to tell God how to do His business. I would pray over the matter, then leave the results and timing to Him. To tell you the truth, I had kind of forgotten about the list until that summer when the words came back again, seemingly out of nowhere.

"Pay attention" seemed to be a repeated mantra in my mind that summer as God began to reopen my heart and call to my remembrance that impossible wish list I'd made a decade earlier. He reminded me of the many promises that accompany our delight in Him. As Norm and I spent more time together, I remember thinking that here was a man who loved the Lord wholeheartedly. He was a self-taught guitar player, who had a wonderful way of making me laugh. One by one the check marks came. Though it wasn't an audible voice, God was speaking. "Pay attention" came to my mind more often than I wanted to admit. I was beginning to understand why.

Norm and I were about as opposite as they come. But those initial weeks of working together to achieve his goals for the class project quickly grew into a friendship we both seemed to enjoy. Being around Norm just felt comfortable, natural; it was like coming home.

Our mutual love of sports, overlapping friendships, and common experiences served as mortar for the foundation we felt emerging. We had each worked as counselors at youth camps for several summers. For years Norm had been a volunteer with Young Life, a Christian organization designed to help high school students develop their relationships with Christ. While teaching school, I had served as a youth and music director in several churches. It was uncanny hearing how many places our stories had crisscrossed.

About midsummer, Norm wanted to say thank you for all the help I had given him in completing his project, so he offered to cook steaks with all the trimmings. We grilled rib eyes, baked a couple of potatoes, and tossed a large salad. Eating by candlelight, we soaked in the sights and sounds of families around the courtyard pool, just steps away from my apartment's open sliding-glass doors.

After dinner we put some records on and sat cross-legged on the shag carpet. The smells of newly mowed grass hung in the summer air and accompanied our discussion of how to put our final touches on his last project. In the middle of that discussion, Anne Murray's hit single "Could I Have This Dance for the Rest of My Life?" began. It was my favorite song, and I'm sure my face lit up in recognition.

As if he had it all planned out, Norm got to his feet, looked down at me with a confident grin, and held out his hand. On cue, I stood and without a word put my hand in his for the first time. I don't think my feet ever touched the floor as we moved slowly over my living room at sunset. That first kiss at the end of the song must have given both of us some answers. At any rate, it was safe to say that my "No Trespassing" sign came down after that. And with its removal, new and different prayers began.

During the next few weeks, our goal became to stuff as many experiences as possible into the little time we had left before Norm left for graduate school. We packed a picnic basket several times for day trips to the quaint, little mountain town of Waynesville, North Carolina, to visit the church where Norm had served as youth minister for a couple of summers.

On one of those trips, Norm brought his guitar along. As the sun painted late-afternoon pictures across our distance view, we feasted on cold cuts and fruit while sitting high up on a grassy pasture hill accompanied by a few grazing cows and scurrying squirrels.

The book of Genesis details God's infinite power and creative wisdom. On the day He made the animals, there is a picture that has always been one of my favorite parts of the creation story. It says, "Then God said, 'Let the earth produce every sort of animal, each producing offspring of the same kind—livestock, small animals that scurry along the ground, and wild animals.' And that is what happened. God made all sorts of wild animals, livestock, and small animals, each able to produce offspring of the same kind. And God saw that it was good" (Genesis1:24–25).

That night little creatures galore scurried along the ground, on the hillsides, and in the trees, adding antics and sweetness to our mountain sunset memory.

As the remaining weeks clicked by, our time together became almost constant. Of course, there was that nervous first trip to meet his parents. Being in his hometown made me think I was strolling through Mayberry. And when we drove up the long drive to his home outside of town, Barney Fife's police cruiser parked in his parents' driveway, minus the light and siren, was more confirmation.

The weekend was laced with what I felt sure were spiced-up war stories of back in the day. Story after side-splitting story seemed to jockey for position that weekend. Tales were spun of how Norm and his older brother launched bottle rockets across Old Orchard Road, sometimes underneath unsuspecting cars. Insane antics he, his brother, and his cousins had somehow pulled off without someone getting arrested or killed flowed from Norm and his parents for three days.

Who would have guessed? This mild-mannered, aspiring pastor was a wild man. One could only imagine what exploits lay ahead for him and his fellow prankster, Kelvin, with the Wild West as their playground. Every part of that weekend served to paint a clearer, more three-dimensional picture of this man I was quickly getting to know.

And perhaps my favorite memory that summer was of Norm, the handsome mystery fan, sitting alone in the bleachers when he came to cheer me on at many of my softball games and regional tournaments. Whether I was catching a fly ball, sliding into second, or stepping up to the plate, his was often the only voice I heard among the crowd.

It all equaled jam-packed, nonstop weeks in which God seemed to be knitting our hearts together in record time. And we both knew it.

Summer ended with Norm passing those dreaded classes with flying colors and my being there for his graduation from Gardner-Webb University. Before leaving for graduate school in the fall, the only tasks left were packing the car and tying up a few last-minute loose ends.

That left the two of us sitting at Wendy's as his departure drew near and needing to make an inevitable, somewhat-dreaded decision.

What, if anything, came next? Long-distance relationships, we were told, were hard and seldom worked out. People said they required too much energy and effort.

"So, where are we going from here?" Norm asked bluntly that afternoon while we shared a chocolate Frosty and a large order of fries.

"I don't know about you, but I'm going back to my apartment when we're done here," I said, feeling my oats since our team had just won a hotly contested softball game.

"No, you know what I mean. We have to decide what we want from this relationship. And more importantly, I think, we need to decide where we want it to go from here." It was an uncharacteristically serious response to my feeble attempt to lighten things.

After a long back-and-forth acknowledging the emotional and distance obstacles that would most likely lie ahead, we decided what we felt for each other wasn't just a passing summer romance. We weighed all the pros and cons of the options that seemed to loom before us.

We didn't know whether what we felt warranted a "true love" label yet, but we had a hunch it was pretty close. Sitting in the booth, we determined that continuing our relationship would be worth the long-distance effort and imminent hurdles. We decided to go for it. We would write, call, and keep in touch. Only time would tell whether God would continue to knit our hearts together over the miles as He had done in the quick passing of that fun-packed, almost magical summer.

Looking back on that day, our hand-in-hand exit from Wendy's actually symbolized an entrance. It would become a God-directed doorway into a journey of walking by faith and learning to trust both God and each other in a thousand new ways. It marked the beginning of an adventure that, like all great epics, would be full of unpredictable twists and unexpected corners. What lay ahead were obstacles and challenges that would require more courage, trust, and perseverance than either of us had at the time.

The Lord says, "I will guide you along the best pathway for your life. I will advise you and watch over you."

—Psalm 32:8

chapter 2

Learning to Expect the Unexpected

The next few months brought the usual long-distance relationship challenges. I learned soon after he left for seminary that Norm had previously dated one of my friends from college. During an unexpected visit to my apartment, she informed me that the man we had both dated was a "heartbreaker extraordinaire." She proceeded to recount examples of young, forlorn women, including herself, whom Norm had loved and left on the proverbial floor.

"Denise, the number of girls he dated on campus probably outnumbered the ones he didn't," she said. I detected an undertone of both sarcasm and warning in her words. Trying to save me from her own heartache, she had come to urge me to proceed with caution, if I dared proceed at all.

Her story took me by surprise and planted more than a few seeds of suspicion about this laid-back young man I was getting to know and had said my teary goodbyes to only a few weeks earlier. Isn't it funny how seeds of doubt are sewn and how they look and grow a lot more like weeds than flowers the deeper you go in relationships?

And it really didn't help matters at all when I learned through a conversation with another mutual friend who attended seminary with Norm that he had already been seen at several events with the daughter of the seminary president. He had only been there a few weeks. At least he aimed high.

Will I become just another in his heartbreak wake? Will I meet the same fate as my friend? I wondered. Thankfully, we were just at the beginning of this relationship, and I wouldn't have my heart totally devastated if President's Daughter was his newest choice. *But do I have to find out through someone else?* I reasoned. Perhaps I had just misunderstood what he meant in our Wendy's conversation. Perhaps the naysayers were right. Dating long distance was indeed too much work, and he had already thrown in the towel.

In our next—shall we say—terse phone conversation, he assured me that there was nothing to the rumors. He and the president's daughter were simply friends, neither of whom wanted to attend school events alone.

Hmmm. Okay, fine. We had dated only a few weeks, and I certainly had no real say in what he did over a thousand miles away. Yes, we had been duly warned. Long-distance relationships were hard work. Ours wouldn't be the exception. It was kind of like learning to dance, only long distance. You can hear the music and the instructor's words, but figuring out where to put your arms and feet can be painfully awkward with taunting giggles from the peanut section of your mind.

But in the banter and bumps of those first few months, our letters crisscrossed the country weekly, and our phone conversations grew longer. By December, we realized we were learning some pretty decent long-distance dance moves. Christmas break couldn't come fast enough.

Then in February, guess who appeared as my much-anticipated Valentine's Day surprise? How could he have known then that I absolutely hate surprises? That cold day, I sauntered, hungry and whipped, into my apartment after a long day of fifth-grade Valentine's Day parties and too much candy. If you know ten-year-olds, you know that particular holiday has more than enough drama to go around.

My best friend and roommate, Marti, a fellow teacher, was his enabler, airport shuttle, and grinning partner in crime. Sipping her hot tea, she knowingly heard and watched the surprise unfold from behind her book on the sofa. I trudged upstairs to my bedroom to unload the pile of books and the papers I had to grade. As I rounded the corner, I saw a smiling man in a bright sweater and jeans sitting on my bed. In a state of shock, I turned to run in silent slow motion as a hundred thoughts swirled in my head.

How could he be sitting right there in my apartment? We had just talked late the night before, and he had definitely been in his dorm room in Fort Worth. I know it was Kelvin's voice I had heard in the background. And Norm had detailed how I should receive the *big* box he had assured me would arrive on Valentine's Day. Well, it had arrived all right. There it was, sitting cross-legged on my bed in all his glory, grinning from ear to ear and not uttering a word. He managed only a sheepish grin and his signature wave.

With a hands-over-mouth scream, I fled from the room and was followed downstairs by the two culprits. Norm and Marti found me in a puddle of tears in a kitchen corner.

His shock-and-awe hilarious reception notwithstanding, we had an unforgettably romantic Valentine's weekend. It quickly became the envy of my friends as I recounted—well, maybe even embellished—it in the days that followed.

Then in late spring, we couldn't deny we were pretty crazy about each other. Somewhere over that previous year, we had gone from deepening friendship to real love. The butterflies-in-your-stomach kind of love. Serious discussions on marriage had come up a few times. Sometimes we discussed the whole idea and institution of marriage theoretically, and if we discussed it with us in the picture, we ended it with "Maybe someday, but it can't happen anytime soon."

"Someday" seemed necessarily a long way off. Norm had to focus on finishing his graduate work. He had no savings and had a part-time job. His parents had generously helped pay all his college tuition fees and were doing the same to help him finish seminary.

Then, during one of our long-distance, late-night phone conversations, Norm threw me a real curveball. "Will you pray about moving to Fort Worth?" he asked as if he were asking what time it was. "Before you say anything, just listen. I've thought about it. I think if you moved to Fort Worth, we could actually date each other. You know, get to see each other more than just holidays when everything is so planned and perfect."

"Norm, I just got my tenure. I love my job and my life here. Now would not be the time to resign. What would my students do if I leave? They would feel abandoned. I don't think you know what you're asking," I said, almost in one breath.

He continued, "I really don't believe we can make a sound decision about our future after having only written letters and talked over the phone. You know that all our dating has been kind of like glitter and magic, like those few weeks we had last summer and then the quick Christmas and Valentine's holidays. The rest has been long distance. We're discussing marriage, but how can we be so sure?"

His question hung in the air like mist on the mountain. He was convinced that if I moved to Fort Worth and found a job, we could see each other more often, really get to know each other, and together prayerfully determine whether our getting married was indeed the next step. Since we both knew we were playing for keeps, his request seemed both logical and practical to him. He seemed pretty determined that I should at least consider the possibility.

But for me it wasn't that simple. After three years of teaching, I had just received tenure as a teacher in the North Carolina public school system. That was a big deal and a milestone I had worked hard to achieve. My reputation as a teacher had taken time to establish. It meant a lot that parents were now requesting me as their child's teacher for the following school year. That was something I didn't take lightly.

After all, I had dedicated years to be where I was. I loved teaching. My students were my joy. With church activities, softball at a serious level, close friends and family nearby, and my teaching career now firmly ensconced, my life felt full and comfortable. I couldn't imagine being anywhere else. The very thought of moving halfway across the country and knowing almost no one wasn't even slightly appealing.

"I will pray about it. But I'm not moving to Fort Worth right now. It makes no sense," I said as our tone changed, and we wrenched ourselves off the phone. I switched off the light and rolled over, but my wordsmith brain churned out a hundred reasons why there would be no move and why my answer would be more emphatic tomorrow night. Each perfectly worded reason played a little more colorfully and sounded more convincing than the one before it.

Then the next day, after sharing my earth-shatteringly ridiculous option with some friends and fellow teachers, I realized an unexpected crack in my resolve. "What? You're going to say no to an opportunity for love and adventure from a hunky young man who's obviously gaga over you? So, when do you think you'll have an opportunity like this one again?" they asked, sounding more like parents than friends.

My moving to Texas sounded like a romantic, Wild West rodeo adventure to them. And living the single teacher's life into infinity in North Carolina paled in comparison to the picture they painted. Their convincing speeches came in envious Technicolor as we sat on work tables in an after-school classroom.

Their attentive curiosity and our further conversation swept me into a new realm of unexpected thinking and deliberating. And their reasoning and artistry served to create more complicated questions. Now, I had a wrestling match of a different kind.

While I had agreed to go anywhere God wanted me to go, I had imagined it would involve giraffes and jungles, not traffic jams and Texas-sized challenges. The questions lined up. They demanded answers.

Who would take my place and go the extra mile for those upcoming fifth-graders? What if I couldn't find a teaching job in Fort Worth? Did I really want to leave my friends and my comfy life in the sleepy little town of Shelby? What would people think of me? Who would take my place on the Gaffney Diamonds softball team? What if this small-town girl couldn't make it in a big city like Fort Worth? What if …

But there was one big question that kept me up at night. What if I gave up everything I had worked so hard for, moved to Fort Worth, and then realized we weren't right for each other? What then?

I felt like David when he faced his giant. Mine was called Fear, and it was flanked by his brother, Panic, that day. Though I had asked

God numerous times to help me slay those giants, they threatened to overwhelm me as I churned out all the reasons why a move right then would be suicidal.

I had read of many instances where God told people to pray and wait for an answer. Jesus urged His disciples to pray, believing God heard and had the power and will to help His children. There were many examples in the Bible of people coming to a crossroads and asking God to direct their steps.

So, after a lot of wrestling, I decided I would do what Gideon did. Gideon was a character in the Bible whose story I had known from childhood. He had a difficult decision to make. So he set out a fleece and made specific requests of God for an answer to his dilemma, using a sheepskin. Even though I could have named scores of real-life situations where God hadn't answered someone's request for a visible sign, I decided, after praying and searching the Bible for answers, that I needed to ask, seek, and knock boldly. So that's what I did.

My fleece, I decided, would be threefold. It needed to be clear, measurable, and practical. If God wanted me to move to Fort Worth (I was pretty sure He didn't),

1. I needed an apartment or house before I got there, and I asked that it be furnished, since this was, after all, a trial move;
2. I needed a full-time job secured before I would even consider resigning my teaching position in North Carolina;
3. And lastly, I asked that the house would have a swing because swinging had been therapy for me all my life, especially on tire swings tied to old oak trees.

Yeah, I know. My requests were brazen. But my fleece came because I really did believe God meant it when He said, "Trust in the Lord with all your heart; do not depend on your own understanding. Seek his will in all you do, and, he will show you which path to take" (Proverbs 3:5–6).

"All right, I agree to pray about what you asked. I will choose to be open to the idea of moving to Texas," I told Norm as we later discussed the whole idea more sanely.

I informed him of my fleece and the three specific requests. We agreed to pray for God's will to be done and for Him to make it clear. I also agreed to fly to Fort Worth to check out job and housing possibilities over his spring break, since Norm would be on a church planting team all summer. That meant he would have little time to help me with my decision. It looked more and more like it was just me and God on this one.

"Keep on asking, and you will receive what you ask for. Keep on seeking, and you will find. Keep on knocking, and the door will be opened to you. For everyone who asks, receives. Everyone who seeks, finds. And to everyone who knocks, the door will be opened. You parents, if your children ask for a loaf of bread, do you give them a stone instead? Or if they ask for a fish, do you give them a snake? Of course not! So if you, sinful people, know how to give good gifts to your children, how much more will your heavenly Father give good gifts to those who ask him."
—Matthew 7:7–11

chapter 3

Should I Stay, or Should I Go?

Spring break in Fort Worth was pedal to the metal from the minute I got off the plane. Doing job interviews, weeding out possible housing options, taking sightseeing trips, and squeezing in as much time with Norm as possible filled seven wonderful days.

I quickly learned more than I really wanted to know about the best and worst places to live in south Fort Worth. I think I was surprised that those days whet my appetite for the possibilities that just might lie ahead. It's funny how God uses experiences and possibilities to fan a flicker in our hearts. Several mission trips while in college had put me on a path toward ministry. It seemed He was doing a similar thing with my exploratory trip to Fort Worth. I sensed God had more for me there. He began stirring the waters in my heart.

Arriving back home, I began the prayerful task of combing through three-by-five cards with the names, addresses, and phone numbers of possible furnished houses and apartments as well as following up on several job interviews that looked promising.

One of the first houses on my list was one on Seminary Drive. It was only a mile from the graduate campus where Norm lived. Across the street from both an elementary school and a city park, it was a perfect setting and location. The woman who answered the phone sounded surprised and a bit irritated as I told her the reason for my call.

"How did you get my number this early?" she asked. "It wasn't supposed to be posted until late July." It wasn't the response I was hoping for, but soon it made sense.

Her irritation melted a bit as she explained that she would be moving to Grand Prairie to care for her son and his family because his wife had terminal leukemia. The couple had two young sons, who needed their grandmother at this most difficult time. She spoke with a candor and emotion I hadn't expected. I learned as we talked further that her son was a busy pastor and desperately needed daily help. Her move, however, wasn't scheduled until late August or September. She had asked the seminary housing office to hold that posting until July. The information I had been given was released weeks before the date she had anticipated. As she talked, it became clear why she had seemed so taken aback by my call.

After answering her question and sharing how I now held her information card, her voice warmed. I got the feeling there was a sprout or two of trust emerging from the ground of our frosty beginning. We decided to talk further over the weekend. The next time we spoke, she seemed to have warmed a little more. She even seemed ready for details about me, my experiences, and the reasons for my potential move.

That conversation felt a little like a job interview. But I put myself in her place and quickly realized it was totally understandable that she seemed quite curious, if not a little skeptical, of this unexpected caller from North Carolina, who potentially would be renting her home.

Mrs. Kendall cut right to the chase. She made it clear she was looking for a responsible, single, career woman. Understandably she required someone up to the task of caring for her home. I heard her concern as she described a lovely home full of memories, fine furniture, and treasured heirlooms. With as much candor, patience, and respect as I could, I answered each of her questions. That conversation ended better than I had expected.

Over the next few weeks, we talked often. We both committed the whole situation to prayer. During that waiting time, I was offered two teaching positions and one job as a private interpreter for the deaf with a school system near Fort Worth. I could hardly believe that not only were my prayers being answered, but I actually had choices.

As the weeks clicked away, Mrs. Kendall and I developed a sweet friendship. She commented to me at one point that I seemed like family. I admitted I felt the same. I don't think she even talked to anyone else about renting her home. But there was just one more question for her before I could make a final decision. My fleece was still the determining factor, and there was a missing piece.

"Mrs. Kendall," I said as the summer drew to a close, "I know this will sound a bit weird, but I need to ask you one more question."

"Okay, honey," she said as I gathered my nerve.

"Would there happen to be a swing anywhere in your yard?"

Wait patiently for the Lord. Be brave and courageous. Yes, wait patiently for the Lord.

—Psalm 27:14

chapter 4

Now for the Hard Part

Solomon says in Ecclesiastes that God has set eternity in the hearts of men. I think that means that deep in mankind's soul there is the knowledge that there is something bigger than us, seeds of longing, of searching for truth, and of connecting to the things beyond the here and now. We are all longing for heaven and the meaning of life, which urges us on into our journey toward God.

Like Solomon states, my love for, and belief in, God was as if it were set before I was born. Kind of like breathing, I truly cannot remember a time when I didn't believe in God and take refuge in the knowledge that He was somehow with me. Deep in my child's heart, I believed in God and sensed He cared about me. From my mother's nightly readings from our family's big, white leather-bound picture Bible with the gold leaf pages, I learned almost every major story of both Old and New Testaments at an early age.

Those vivid stories and my own insatiable, questioning curiosity of God and nature gave me and my three brothers a rich foundation for our faith. All four of us made the decision to follow Christ before turning ten. Like icing on the cake, all the richness and blessings of being raised on a farm gave that faith lots of fertile soil to emerge and grow in. That foundation set my feet on the path of a private journey with God. That journey has grown more precious and meaningful with each passing year.

Through the simple joys and pain I experienced as a child, to the many pivotal moments of those awkward, painfully insecure teenage years, my faith in God was more than just an anchor. God was the strong, faithful Refuge to which I often retreated, and He was the One with whom I had walked my whole life. Talking to God had always come like breathing.

So when Norm asked me to move to Fort Worth, I quickly became aware that the easy part was telling him I would pray about the decision.

It wasn't like I had put the fleece out with no fear or trepidation. I had known all too well from real life experiences and from studying and teaching the Bible for years that God didn't always honor someone's request for a sign. He usually leads us by faith without tangible signs. Truth be known, I would have most likely counseled anyone in my situation to do just the opposite. I would have said, "Don't be so presumptuous and brazen with God. Even Jesus, when tempted in the desert, told Satan that he should not test God like that."

But there it was. Before me lay a specific list of requests and beside it some pretty undeniably specific answers. The hard part was coming to terms with what now stared us in the face. One by one each request I had prayed for had been answered, except for one little detail.

Now if I truly believed God heard and answered prayer, and if I really knew He had a good plan for my future, then I needed to put my money where my mouth was. It was time. I had taught Bible studies, assuring friends that God wanted to show them His will even more than they wished to know it. I had sung that old hymn a thousand times.

Trust and obey,
For there's no other way,
To be happy in Jesus,
But to trust and obey.

But that was while I was standing on a church pew, trying to sing harmony with my best friend, Becky. This was real life. And before me lay a real, life-changing, never-going-back-again kind of trusting and obeying with actual consequences.

One more question lingered. I had to know its answer.

Mrs. Kendall's reply didn't really surprise me when I asked her that day about the swing. Everything else on my list had been checked off.

"Why, yes. How did you know? There's a tire swing on a long rope in the backyard. My husband put that thing up years ago for our grandchildren."

"I just had a feeling there would be a tire swing in your yard," I said as I explained to her my story of the fleece. Tears flowed over the dam that had been holding them back for weeks. Change was inevitable for us both. Our long silence over the miles spoke clearly what words couldn't.

After a few more back-and-forth wrestling matches with God over all the "what if's" and insanity of moving halfway across the country with absolutely no guarantees, I realized there really was a nudging deep inside I knew well as the voice of God. There were undeniable hedges directing me toward a door that opened into a new room of that house I had asked God to build for me. Something was pulling me from my comfortable life, urging me toward a new place that required trust. Would I swing the door open and cross this unusual threshold? There was just enough light to see where to put my feet next. That was all I had. But that same voice allayed my fears and gave me assurance that the limited light was all I needed for now.

By summer's end, I resigned my newly tenured fifth-grade teaching position. I accepted the job as interpreter for the deaf near Fort Worth. And I told Mrs. Kendall I would take really good care of her special home while she was away, caring for her sweet family, who needed her so desperately. She seemed elated about my coming and began preparing me with a list of details I would need to take care of before taking the house keys.

I began the dreaded task of packing up and saying goodbye to everything and everyone I had known for twenty-five years. The most difficult of all my goodbyes, except of course to my family and best friend, would be to my students.

They had been my life for more than three years and were whom I had planned my every day around. I was one of those teachers who was all in. My students were both the joys and frustrations of almost every weekday conversation. And the frustrations, in reality, came from my often-feeble attempts to help them reach more of their God-given potential than they were willing or able to give.

More stories than I could count flashed through my mind, stories of students in whom I had poured my life as they grew and learned beyond what anyone thought possible as the school years progressed. They were the treasures I would never forget. I loved teaching and had never wanted to do anything else … except be a mother someday.

Each class had proved unique and memorable. As part of the fabric of my life, I felt the huge rip as I said goodbye. The belief or maybe hope that there would be other classrooms full of kids who needed a teacher in Texas kept my feet moving and brought a tiny measure of comfort.

As I navigated through all the emotion of closing that chapter I held so dear, I had no idea that right around the corner awaited one more lavish confirmation. It would be a bit of icing on the cake that Norm and I could never have orchestrated or thought to put on a list. But isn't that often what the goodness of God looks like?

The faithful love of the Lord never ends!
His mercies never cease.
Great is his faithfulness;
his mercies begin afresh each morning.
                            —Lamentations 3:22–23

chapter 5

A Bit More Icing on the Cake

While for me that second summer simmered with one rapid realization after the next that my prayers were being heard and answered, Norm's days teemed with activity and opportunities to serve and grow in his internship near Plymouth, Michigan.

As the summer drew to a close, his parents invited me to drive to Michigan with them to bring Norm home. I jumped at the chance to see where he had spent his summer and was grateful beyond words to have an opportunity to get to know them better as well.

We packed as much sightseeing as possible into that long weekend. The entire Detroit area was full of fascinating history. Our tour of the Henry Ford Museum and Greenfield Village in Dearborn was the highlight for me.

Seeing the tiny space where Norm had lived all summer was the biggest surprise of the weekend. His parents and I stood in shock and amazement when we entered the front door. That apartment was more like a travel trailer than the efficiency the newspaper had touted. The guys didn't seem to give it a second thought. "It was bigger and better than sleeping in a tent all summer," Norm said as he gave us the nickel tour. Now that was true. Perspective is everything.

The best part for me was their impossible-to-stand-up-in dormer bathroom with a showerhead about as high as their waists that Norm, at six two, and his even taller co-worker, Pete, had somehow squeezed and ducked into that entire muggy summer. I think it kept them laughing and looking forward to getting back to the luxury of their dorm rooms.

On our way home, we stopped at a Denny's restaurant for breakfast. While finishing our Grand Slam platters, we noticed a distinguished, silver-haired gentleman sitting alone across the room. I guessed him to be a successful businessman from the pleat in his suit, perhaps in his early seventies.

Finishing his breakfast with one last sip of coffee, he folded his paper, picked up his ticket, and came directly to our table to ask directions, thinking we must be locals. He introduced himself and reached out to shake our hands.

"Good morning my name is Clyde Mull and I am looking for a little tool and dye shop that must be near here. Being from Dallas, I have no idea where this place is." He pulled out the card with the address he was looking for.

My mouth must have been gaping as I heard his words. "Excuse me, but did you say Clyde Mull?" I asked.

"Yes, that's right," he said.

"That's amazing because my daddy's name is Clyde Mull," I said and explained that we were also just passing through. Norm and I stared at each other, trying not to embarrass the man. You could have blown me over with a feather.

It wasn't exactly a John Smith kind of name. My request for clarity came out with a burst of enthusiasm that surprised even me. Noticeably taken aback, he grew more attentive as I asked questions, and we began a more in-depth conversation about how amazing it was that our paths happened to cross there in Michigan.

I explained that my family lived in North Carolina. Immediately hearing the Carolina connection, our new friend looked almost as incredulous as I felt.

As the conversation unfolded, we learned that he and his wife had recently begun a genealogy search, which included family they had located in the Carolinas. Could we be related? He warmed quickly, and our back-and-forth conversation now filled the restaurant with laughter and new, enthusiastic curiosity.

When he learned Norm was in seminary in Fort Worth and that I was planning on moving there in the fall, there blossomed an instant interest and genuine endearment that is difficult to describe. Just a few minutes either way would have rendered our meeting a nonentity, and we knew it.

We exchanged contact information as we shook hands and exited Denny's. "Now here's my card. It has our address and my phone number on it. I want you two to give me a call as soon as you get settled in Fort Worth. Dorothy and I would love it if you could come for dinner," he said as he shared a few details about how to find his Dallas neighborhood.

Well, what do you know? This handsome, distinguished stranger, who moments ago had sat pensively alone while studying his *Wall Street Journal* over coffee, had just become a kind, generous friend, neighbor, and perhaps even a relative. We were flabbergasted as we walked to our car. All we could say for the next hour was, "What are the odds?" or "Can you believe what just happened? If we had stopped at that rest station beforehand, we would have missed all that."

The Bible teaches that God cares for us and that He knows everything about us. He even knows the number of hairs on our heads. His love for us is often more extravagant than we expect or think we deserve. You could never convince me that we had just experienced an unexplainable accident. How could we have known then that this *chance* meeting in Plymouth, Michigan, would yield to me such rich grace wrapped in arms of love in a place where I knew no one but Norm? How could I have known then how significant that meeting would be in our story?

The rest of our journey home from Michigan seemed uneventful after that, except perhaps that it was on our way home when Norm and I had our first major disagreement. It was a silly back-and-forth over my wanting "just a bite" of his chocolate Frosty. "I asked if you wanted one of your own," was his short response to my quickly recoiled request.

I moved closer to my side of the car and nursed a newfound interest in mile after monotonous mile of plants, and highway signage.

Needing a good pout for being denied my wish, my heels dug in as we traveled along in thick silence with his parents in the back seat unaware of the drama playing out up front.

Selfishness. Control. Making quick mountains out of molehills. Punitive silence. We both felt the unquenchable need to be right and that we were entitled to better treatment. Even then we sought the impossible from each other. Neither of us saw the implications of that moment. How could we? We were young, obliviously in love, and didn't know what we didn't know.

We arrived home a bit road weary, and by then had kissed and made up. All was well with the world. I began the inevitable tasks of last-minute packing, purging, tying up a gazillion loose ends, and saying those dreaded goodbyes.

Driving those long stretches of Interstates 85 and 20 alone in my brand-new gray Pontiac, which bulged with all my earthly goods, I kept Norm's 280-Z taillights in constant view through that teary, doubt-filled thousand-mile journey to my new home on West Seminary Drive in Fort Worth, Texas. In my bones, I ached with the awareness that life as I had known it was now in my rearview mirror. I kept comforting myself with hollow words that a new, "exciting" adventure lay somewhere beyond my headlights.

But for some reason, that entire second road trip seemed more full of fear and second-guessing myself than anything else. Those familiar what-ifs had now become monsters in my head that required a frequent rehearsal of God's promises of faithfulness to me. I also recalled for mile after silent mile, as if in a dream, all those specifically answered prayers over that mind-boggling, miracle-filled year.

"For I know the plans I have for you," says the Lord. "They are plans for good and not for disaster, to give you a future and a hope. In those days when you pray, I will listen. If you look for me wholeheartedly, you will find me."

—*Jeremiah 29:11–13*

chapter 6

Seismic Paradigm Shifts

More difficult and yet more life changing than I could ever have anticipated, my move to Fort Worth began with fireworks. My new job as private interpreter for the deaf turned out to be a harrowing experience.

One of my students had a well-deserved title of "Holy Terror." Apparently, she regarded it a badge of honor. Her long résumé of offenses began with severe cruelty to animals, physically and verbally assaulting several faculty members, and refusing to even look in the direction of her interpreter. A few of the staff informed me of her abusive home life, explosive anger, and sadistic behavior patterns. Several other interpreters had resigned in less than two years over their volatile dealings with her. Despite all our student-teacher conferences and efforts, answers evaded everyone involved. My resolve to never give up proved futile. Norm and I agreed our relationship had been greatly impacted by the unrelenting emotional rollercoaster I had been on, and by semester's end, I too tendered my resignation.

Within a few weeks I gratefully accepted a fifth-grade teaching position at a private academy in Arlington. It was an unusually seamless transition; I missed no work, and my new position began the next semester. With a thousand times less stress, a surprisingly familiar curriculum, and a classroom full of eager students, I felt right at home. Thankful I was able to once again just teach and share stories with ten-year-olds, I jumped in with both feet. From that point on, my outlook and energy toward life in Fort Worth improved steadily, and I began to embrace my new home and the journey it promised.

Pretty soon Norm and I developed routines. We enjoyed game nights, attended Bible studies, and got together for dinners with friends from seminary. God was teaching me to push beyond my fears and insecurities and just get involved in others' lives.

Most of the people Norm introduced me to were newly married couples or singles he knew from graduate school. Many of them lived in seminary housing or in the dorms. Norm and I saw up close and personal that it didn't take much money to have rich evenings filled with all kinds of food, laughter, and creativity that yielded deep conversations and lasting memories.

By this time, we had successfully turned our frustration-fraught, long-distance romance into an actual dating relationship. We hammered out a weekly rhythm of work, play, church life, and school that served to let us really get to know and experience each other in the everyday stuff of life.

It was in Fort Worth that God began to shine a bigger light on my pride and narrow-mindedness. I knew the verse about God's thoughts being higher than our thoughts, but I thought mine usually came pretty close. In His faithfulness to make me into His likeness, He began to give me glimpses of how myopic and small my view of the world was. In His mercy, He opened my eyes to the fact that I knew so little about Him, and what He was up to in the world. I had a feeling many much-needed paradigm shifts loomed on the horizon for this small-town Carolina girl. My past met my future in Fort Worth. Everything I had learned and assumed as a child came under scrutiny.

From childhood our local church had been a huge influence in my life. Our pastor and his wife were some of my heroes for almost as long as I can remember. I was never anything but grateful for the sound Bible teaching I received there. At nine I made a personal decision to follow Jesus and asked Him to forgive my sin and guide my life. I was baptized on Easter Sunday soon after that.

I am eternally thankful for all the wonderful older members of our church, many of whom took me under their wing and encouraged my new faith. Their relationships with God and knowledge of scripture challenged me to study and memorize Bible passages. I attended weekly Sunday school classes, worship services, Bible studies, and vacation Bible school in the summers.

How well I still remember the fun of games and refreshments on the church lawn after youth group. Special-occasion potlucks featured the best cooks on earth. They spread tables as far as the eye could see with southern fried chicken, mashed potatoes, corn on the cob, fresh green beans, hams, stews, casseroles, homemade pickles and jams, soufflés, yeast rolls, salads, and pies. Cakes of every size and color occupied their own table alongside decadent desserts beyond our wildest chocolate dreams. For some reason marshmallows and coconut flowed freely on potluck Sundays.

Around age nine or ten, I joined an organization called GAs (Girls in Action), which was our denomination's service arm for the girls in youth group. Along with the aim for us to study and apply the Bible to our lives, one of its purposes was to serve needy people in our area. There was an equivalent organization for guys called RAs, which stood for Royal Ambassadors. It trained up young men to know God and the scriptures, and to serve their communities.

In GAs we had opportunities to serve and visit those, including the sick and elderly, in nursing homes, prisons, and our city's two mental health facilities. We saved and gave our money to supply basic supplies, such as toiletries, to missionaries both overseas and here in the States. We learned the value and joys of giving both time and money.

There were various levels of achievement, toward which we could work if we chose. To reach the higher levels in Girls in Action, we had options to read and write summaries of a plethora of biographies of great Christian men and women, and to achieve higher levels of scripture memory and community service. I chose to go to those higher levels and loved every challenging, rewarding minute of it.

To challenge us to know our Bibles well, there were sword drills— so called because the Bible is referred to as the "sword of the Spirit."

During those fun contests, young people from first through eighth or ninth grades who had memorized the locations of all sixty-six books of the Bible would stand at attention, Bibles held at their sides, ready for action. We looked like a ragtag army of soldiers.

Of course, we had practiced for hours at home so we would be ready when we stood at the front of our classrooms or the church for tournaments. It was a competition to see who could locate verses in their Bibles the fastest as a "caller" named a random book and verse for us to locate and read aloud. I remember the fun and the thrill we all felt as we listened for the next command. "Read, set—find Matthew 6:23—go!"

From my many age-mates to the elderly gentlemen and sweet, motherly grannies who faithfully came, served, and worshipped week after week, the lessons I took away from those rich years could fill a book. My church, its pastor, and the expressions of love in our community in Morganton laid a strong foundation, on which God would build and speak for the rest of my life.

Our time in Fort Worth would allow God to merge both our past experiences with His vision for our future. He would build new rooms and entire wings onto an existing foundation. It became clear as we talked about our future in light of our similar past church experiences that the real foundation was Christ. He was the architect of our faith, not a denomination, set of experiences, or traditions.

For the first year, we attended a large church in Fort Worth called Southcliff Baptist Church. Dr. Jack Taylor was its pastor. We grew tremendously there, but sensed the need for a smaller community after a while. That desire triggered our search for sound teaching in a smaller community. We didn't know exactly what we were looking for, but we prayed that God would direct us and help us to know when we had found it.

After months of visiting several churches in the area, we were invited to an exciting new church which met in a YMCA building. A group of about seventy-five met on Sunday evenings. Hope Community Church felt like home from the first visit. At Hope we met all types and ages of people who had such contagious, humble, service-oriented zeal for God and others that our hearts were challenged to consider a new model of how church looked. It was a paradigm shift that would change our lives. Soon it became clear that God had directed us to Hope for many reasons. We joined the church and embraced its mission and vision with a conviction I hadn't experienced before.

It was there too that God put gasoline on an already lit fire in our hearts for studying the Bible, deliberately investing in people, getting to know people through small groups, and learning the value of church planting. These were all gnawing desires we already had but couldn't have articulated until the leaders and members at Hope lived them out day in and day out. They also put those principles into a practical, transparent format we could see, embrace, and learn how to duplicate.

Norm and I witnessed, perhaps for the first time, what it really looked like to lay down our lives for others. At Hope we experienced a genuine community of people serving people in Christ's name. It was a beautiful, humbling, life-altering experience. We continue to feel the impact of our years at Hope and are grateful for the leadership and teaching of our pastor, Harold Bullock, who became mentor, friend, counselor, and vision caster. It was through those formative years in Fort Worth that Norm and I chose to give our lives to sharing the love of Christ with others and helping them grow in their faith, whatever form that took and wherever that commitment might lead us. As we look back, we see how God used those years to instill convictions and life principles that would impact every arena of our lives.

Experiencing all those new beginnings, struggling with jobs, defining and refining calling and purpose, serving together for the first time in a church, and seeing up close and weekly each other's strengths, weaknesses, and responses under pressure brought clarity to many of our questions. Evidence of that clarity came in mid-December.

The evening began as a fun adventure date to an undisclosed location. All I had been told was to dress for a special night out.

Norm insisted I wear a blindfold. As he drove, we laughed and talked for over an hour on what I assumed was a freeway.

With humorous instruction, Norm led me through a parking lot and into what felt and sounded like a grand hotel or office tower. It was our first faith walk. He led me to an elevator and selected the floor. Seconds later, as the elevator doors opened, I could hear dinner music and smell steaks, seafood, and hollandaise, so I surmised our surroundings were upscale and expensive.

With the blindfold removed, my eyes adjusted and filled with awe as I drank in the modern beauty of steel and glass etched against an evening sky. I recognized it as the top floor of the famous Reunion Tower in Dallas. It was the same view panned every week in the intro of the television drama *Dallas*. We had been to the restaurant once before, but as students we had just browsed around nonchalantly, asked to see a menu, and slunk back to the elevators without making a scene.

Now, somehow here we were. Adorned with upscale southwest Christmas class, it was a beautiful revolving restaurant, which allowed us to drink in the sparkle of the entire Dallas skyline silhouetted against the orange and reds of a bold Texas sunset. My date, with hands in his pockets, seemed to revel in my every sign of surprise and wonder. A flawless plan well executed began our evening to remember. As the moon soon took center stage on the panorama, our conversation lingered over each course.

It was just before dessert when Norm pulled from his jacket pocket a little cream-colored box with gold edging. After recounting the highlights of our friendship and dating journey to that point, he finally got to the reason for all the drama. With a tenderness that wasn't his trademark, he slowly pushed the box to my side of the table, almost pausing halfway.

"So, April Denise Mull, will you spend the rest of your life with me?"

Words seemed like a cheap response as I opened the box and a perfect solitaire engagement ring sparkled up at me.

I had an idea then that there was quite a story accompanying this ring. A full-time student, Norm had worked at Sears every hour he could. I knew he had no savings to speak of. Later I learned that with the help of his parents and a jeweler friend, a plan had been hatched to buy the ring. And by cobbling together my comments the few times we had browsed jewelry store windows, he had chosen the simple design I had dreamed of.

"Yes, I will," I said with a confidence and joy that surprised even me. Holding hands across the table, I don't remember many tears, but I remember a shiver and then a smiling happiness that spread from head to toe.

Our desserts were delivered, accompanied by kind wishes and excitement from our servers and fellow diners, as I showed off Norm's design. Our engagement evening began and ended in a total surprise. It was a magical moment perfectly planned and brilliantly orchestrated. But wouldn't you know it? Norm still couldn't help but tease me with "You know, honey, I never did actually ask you to marry me."

I wonder whether he planned it that way.

There are three things that amaze me—no, four things that I don't understand: how an eagle glides through the sky, how a snake slithers on a rock, how a ship navigates the ocean, how a man loves a woman.
                                    —Proverbs 30:18–19

chapter 7

Extravagant Grace

Running parallel with all those first few months in Fort Worth was the story of the Mulls. Remember the surprise meeting at Denny's in Michigan? We contacted them soon after getting settled. Their invitation still stood for us to come for dinner. There was an instant bond from that reunion with Mr. Mull in their driveway when we met his wife. Almost instantly their place became our home away from home.

During one of our first visits, we discovered that Mrs. Mull had worked at Joske's of Dallas as the head of their bridal department. After we were engaged, she asked whether she could make my wedding veil since that had been her specialty at Joske's. I learned from people we met that she was the best. She, of course, knew all the little hole-in-the-wall kinds of places in downtown Dallas. She took me to this lovely little corner boutique and helped me pick out the most exquisite Alençon lace. What she designed and created over hours and hours of tedious needlework was an exquisitely elegant, hand-stitched wedding gift I'm to this day unable to describe without tears. Norm and I were the blessed recipients of their kindness, generosity, and amazing friendship over those years.

Their eventual trip to North Carolina in search of kin was an amazing experience for us all. As both Clyde Mulls shook hands and looked each other in the eye, as men of that greatest generation do, I remembered the day at Denny's and thanked God for His gift of friendship.

There was a definite family resemblance. For some reason it didn't surprise us when we discovered the link making us distant cousins. The Mulls were always kind and generous in the ways they shared their lives with Norm and me.

To our total amazement, knowing we were big Cowboy fans, they once even let us use their season tickets with unbelievable seats at a home game. That first ever trip to a professional stadium is a memory time can never fade. And still on display in my china hutch sits a beautiful set of Mrs. Mull's bone china plates and tea cups. They were her gift to me before we moved to Nashville. We treasure those gifts and evenings at their home. It was then that we discovered the way is never long to the house of a friend. The Mulls from Dallas became a joy and source of wise counsel to us for the rest of their lives. Their friendship, generosity, and legacy live on in our hearts today.

There is no greater love than to lay down one's life for one's friends.
—John 15:13

chapter 8

Against All Odds

After our engagement, we decided it would be an investment in our future to hire a premarital counselor. We chose a well-known author who was respected in the area and came highly recommended.

In our first session, we met with him together and filled out several types of personality profiles as homework. Next, we shared our stories with him one-on-one before he began making assessments. Together in his office for his assessments of what he had learned, our jaws and hearts dropped as he voiced his conclusions.

"Well, Norm and Denise, to tell you the truth, I have never counseled a couple any more opposite on just about every level than you guys." He paused to let that sink in. Then he continued with a solemn tone. "I am not saying it's impossible, but I am saying it's improbable that you guys will stay married long term. With all I've compiled through meetings with you individually and through your profiles, I would urge you to proceed in your marriage plans only if you truly believe this is God's will for you and only if you're willing to face what I believe will be tremendous hurdles." He looked us squarely in the eye.

Was that his standard line to all his clients? I don't know. He sure appeared seriously concerned. Maybe he wanted to sober us, to shake us out of believing the road before us would be all songs and roses. Whatever his reasons, we were all ears.

He continued by laying out in deep, dark detail our major

differences in background, personality, temperament, and communication styles. He described more clearly than we really wanted to hear how our glaring differences would affect how each of us would give and receive information. He described how my wounds from childhood would eventually affect Norm and how Norm's lack of them would give him no such category.

The picture he painted of how, as polar opposites, we would perceive, respond to, and filter conflict was hard hitting and difficult to swallow. In no uncertain terms, he laid out how challenges as big and pronounced as ours usually spelled failure for even the most well-intentioned couples. It quickly became painfully clear that he was simply giving us his professional opinion. He gave us the hard truth and left the decision of whether to move forward to us.

We left his office subdued by his counsel and decided to commit his insights to prayer. I think he was surprised when we chose to continue working through the next few months of counseling. We expressed our gratitude for his warnings, concerns, and expertise, and we plowed through the next five months with eyes and hearts as absorbent as possible.

Looking back, he was right about our being opposite in every way. We knew he wasn't talking about opposites in the sense of how they naturally attract. Our particular set of challenges have at times seemed insurmountable. Our communication styles were obviously poles apart, and our backgrounds and filters often landed us on different planets. My overly sensitive, wounded heart and Norm's lack of words and inability to relate with my background indeed stood as big barriers to connection. But everyone had their challenges and we had glimpses, even then, that God was a God of the impossible. It is truer than we know that He receives more glory when the odds are extreme long shots. After looking at the options and praying for wisdom, we decided to go for it. We would be the long shots.

What is impossible for people is possible with God.
                                                    —*Luke 18:27*

chapter 9

Our Wedding Day

Our wedding day finally came on June 18. We thought sandwiching our wedding day between Norm's birthday and Father's Day would be an easy way to remember our anniversary. It was.

For reasons too numerous to list, that whole day seemed a little like a blur to me. I remember a few things, though. I remember waking up that morning with emotions hounding me from every direction. I can still see my beautiful ivory dress, specially designed and handmade by my Proverbs 31 mother, hanging outside the closet.

A few months earlier, I had detailed my dream dress to Mother from my Texas kitchen. "I want it to be ivory but not too ivory. I tried on a few white ones over in Dallas, and they totally washed me out. Do you remember the pink one you made me when I was in seventh grade and how it fit?" Our conversation continued with me describing the neckline, the puffy sleeves, and the fit and flow. She had drawn a sketch simply from my description over the phone.

Mother had worked day and night to create the perfect dress for her only daughter's special day. And perfect it was, along with the other nine dresses she painstakingly sewed for my bridesmaids on her old faithful Singer sewing machine. Stunning when I think back! I still stand in awe at the tremendous sacrifices and acts of service my parents gave without a thought over all those years.

The special ivory hat Dorothy Mull and I had shopped for was the crowning piece to my wedding gown. She had hand-stitched and attached the Alençon lace, creating an exquisite veil. Though the Mulls from Dallas couldn't make the trip due to health reasons, it overwhelmed me as I realized such tender expressions of love from two precious women both married to a man named Clyde Mull surrounded me on my wedding day.

I remember walking down the aisle on Daddy's strong arm with a lifetime of memories mingled in the tears I somehow held back.

Norm surprised me with an original wedding song written by one of his friends. Just before the prayer portion of the ceremony, Norm sang to me as he played his guitar.

Here are two of the six verses to that song written especially for us:

> You love me, and you'll never let me go.
> You love me, oh how wonderful to know
> That you care for me and you'll share
> With me all your sorrows and your joys.
> I've waited for God's own perfect will.
> I've waited, and He taught me to be still
> And to realize that my life He would fulfill,
> And within your love He made it real.

Our song captured what we had dreamed aloud during those last six months. We had indeed waited. We had waited to give ourselves completely to each other. It was then—and continues to be—a gift we have never regretted, a priceless commodity few in our culture are willing to save for the one they will marry, and one that has grown more precious to us over the years for a multitude of reasons.

So there I stood, looking through tears of joy into the beaming, future-filled eyes of my singing, guitar-playing husband. He was the one for whom I had prayed my whole life, the embodiment of my impossible teenage list. Yes, I was saying, "I do" and "I will" to the God-sent man of my dreams.

We were entering the one human relationship where we have the opportunity to be fully known and fully loved just the way we are, warts and all. Yet it is the one place where we have someone willing to also call us out and encourage us onward toward the person we were meant to be. Marriage is where we can see "now and not yet" on grand display every day—two distinct beings, created in the image of God, calling one another higher up and further in. The marriage union is one of God's great mysteries. Can you think of any other relationship that offers such intimacy, commitment, challenge, and promise?

After the ceremony and short reception, we retrieved our car from the super-secret garage, where it had been safely stashed, foiling the rice showers, spark plug removal, and prank-ready antics of Norm's grinning groomsmen. My now-unassuming-but-spunky mother-in-law had strung several pairs of Norm's old, holey Converse and K-Swiss tennis shoes together and secured them to the bumper of his 280-Z.

She and Dad, along with my parents and a few of our mild-mannered, sane friends, had applied proper amounts of shaving cream, streamers, and signage to our getaway car. So with stars in our eyes, our bikes, and those worn-out shoes bobbing obediently in our rearview mirror, we were finally Hilton Head bound.

After only a few minutes of grateful silence in the car, my tears and emotions spilled over the dam. The day I had dreamed of had come and gone. We were now husband and wife. No longer two but one. Now we would embark on a new journey into discovering what living as one looked like. Out of nowhere, a thousand thoughts rushed in all at once. I cried for the first twenty miles or so, with Norm looking helplessly over at his new bride. "Was it something I said?" he asked again.

"No, it's not you. It's just that my whole past and future hit me at once, honey. I can't talk right now," I said as I turned toward my window. Exhaustion, fear, excitement, joy, praise, curiosity, and then another layer of fear jockeyed for position. Emotions of every color and shape raced from the gate as my past and our future met on this day that marked the end of life as I had known it and the beginning of life with the man of my dreams. Wasn't this supposed to be the happiest day of my life? It was, and it wasn't. It was at once elated and vacant as I looked over for the first time at the driver of our car; my new husband.

God whispered His love and presence into my young heart as I turned again to face the window. I was His child. He was my Father. Today was the day I had dreamed of ever since I could remember. His plans for me were good. His promises rang more clearly in my mind. And with those reassurances that came like so many whispers, my tears of too much emotion trailed off and stopped. Joy returned. Just like that.

"Where do you want to eat tonight, Sweetheart?" I asked the handsome man I had just married.

"Oh, I already have all that figured out." He smiled as he reached for my hand and caught the sparkle in my eye.

"At last!" the man exclaimed. "This one is bone from my bone, and flesh from my flesh! She will be called 'woman,' because she was taken from 'man.'" This explains why a man leaves his father and mother and is joined to his wife, and the two are united into one. Now the man and his wife were both naked, but they felt no shame.
                                                    —Genesis 2:23–25

chapter 10

Now for the Happily-Ever-After Part

I've heard some people say they're still on their honeymoon after ten, twenty, even (like my parents) sixty-three years of marriage. Then again, I've had conversations with friends who woke up after only a few weeks, looked over, and realized the honeymoon was definitely over. Like every pair of newlyweds, our hearts were set on growing old together. So far so good.

After our honeymoon and a couple weeks of just being with family and friends in the Carolinas, we returned to Fort Worth and Mrs. Kendall's home, excited to write our first chapter as husband and wife.

Norm plunged headfirst back into studies and term papers. It was his last semester of graduate school. My teaching continued so I could receive my PHT (Putting Hubby Through) degree.

Our first couple months were blissfully full and relatively easy. We were lovers in love. Then without fanfare or blue lights, the counsel we had received from our marriage counselor about how and why we would struggle began ringing in our ears and making more sense. It soon hit us that being so in love was the fireworks display that had gotten us here, but that staying in love would require something much less tingly, and without a lot of glitz or glamour. Sustaining and growing our marriage would require a love that persisted day in and day out. It had names like commitment, fidelity, faithfulness, and devotion.

I read somewhere that women are like spaghetti and men are like waffles. I think they were on to something. They had been talking about the complexity and diversity of our brains and how men and women think on totally different planes much of the time. The analogy gives us a picture of how those mental patterns or processes either overlap and spin off each other like spaghetti or line up neatly compartmentalized like waffles. In thinking it through, it wasn't a bad word picture.

I'm sure my spaghetti ways began to drive Norm crazy within the first couple months. Take our way of arranging our desks, for instance. I knew exactly where everything was. My piles of things were usually stacked and arranged semi-neatly on my work surface. I always cleared out a space somewhere in the middle. Exactly where was part of the mystery. Most of the time I could visualize the location of everything right in my head. If he needed to see a bill or find a receipt, I would say, "Sure, Sweetie, it's on my desk. Right-hand corner, second pile from the back under the large green envelope."

Within minutes he would emerge around the corner with bill in hand, shaking his head, usually with a glazed look of sheer amazement. He wasn't at all certain how that just happened. Garnering a knowing smile, the glint in my eye meant, *See, you should never doubt me.*

Norm is regimented, dependably on time, and self-disciplined. A natural born organizer, he had a file folder labeled for every paper. Everything was filed as soon as he handled it or shortly thereafter. His socks, shirts, and pants were color coordinated and all lined up in the closet or the dresser drawer. His tools and gadgets in the garage followed suit.

Now there's nothing at all wrong with being organized. Most of us aspire to order. I certainly do. But the problem for us was that Norm's way had become the best way. His way of organizing became our standard, our measuring stick. He believed it, and for whatever reasons, so did I. Under the surface, we both began to live our lives by Norm's right way of doing things.

The waffles-and-spaghetti comparison described us in other ways. I have tried over the years to describe to Norm how my mind never seems to shut down. Being a driven personality, my brain incessantly churns out a hundred eager thoughts at once. In fact, from the time I open my eyes in the morning until my last awareness at night, my mind is producing, creating, ruminating, and planning. Certainly it is never idle. So if Norm asked what I was thinking, it might take a while for me to connect all the dots of my pinball machine thought process. That usually left him dazed. He couldn't understand how I could wind up there from where I'd started.

Norm had no such category. We might be on a road trip when our conversation would go like this:

I would say, "You look like you're deep in thought. What are you thinking, Honey?"

"Nothing," he'd say.

"No, I'm curious, what are your thoughts right now?" I'd say.

"I'm thinking nothing," he would repeat.

"What do you mean, 'Nothing'? You can't be thinking nothing. That's impossible. I never think nothing," I would counter.

"No, for me, it is possible. I'm not thinking about anything. I'm just driving," he would conclude before checking his mirror and changing lanes.

It took years, but I finally got the same answer enough times to know it was true. I would just have to accept it on blind faith. He was thinking nothing.

The topic of finances possibly topped our opposites list. Like most couples, the way we viewed the money we made and our budget became one of the most challenging bones of contention we faced. It became crystal clear during that first trying year or two as man and wife that we were indeed ill equipped to deal with important financial decisions, let alone the pressures of bills with not enough money left at the end of the month.

It became obvious we were just as ill prepared to face the self-centeredness, impatience, stubbornness, and pride we too often witnessed in each other. We became skilled at seeing the log in each other's eye. Blame-shifting, the desperate need to be right, paralyzing expectations, and our failure to anticipate the difficulties were qualities that put us on a path that spelled imminent frustration. We wanted to love perfectly, but found ourselves doing it all wrong. But our intentions were good. Did that count?

It was as though we had carried our "his" and "hers" suitcases into the living room of our marriage and set them down. As we unpacked the contents of those cases, we both discovered items we hadn't remembered packing. One example was our total inability to have a disagreement and stay in the same room to see it through. Week after week, two completely different sets of life experiences, ingrained habits, expectations, wounds, response filters, and communication styles collided like waves in a storm. While it was true those suitcases held enormous potential for growth, we viewed their contents like fingernails on a chalkboard. All those stark differences became instruments which produced painfully long screeching sounds. Like a quiet volcano with molten lava under pressure flowing just beneath the surface, neither of us was aware just when or where the eruptions were about to happen.

As those irritations, coupled with the crescendo of mounting financial pressures grew, so did the number of times we found ourselves longing for the good old days of singleness when the few arguments we had seldom lasted past a pout and a make-up kiss or two. With each frustration, our chasm widened between what we wanted our marriage to look like and what we saw emerging.

That year, my temptation wasn't so much to pack my bags and leave physically as it was to withdraw and build walls emotionally. I admit there were many times I was tempted to close up the shop of my heart and never come back. It became clear that dying to myself and laying down my life for another were concepts easier taught to others than lived out in the context of a committed relationship.

Too often we found ourselves pining for the simple, not so messy days just a few months ago when we could just forget about it, go home, or change the subject. We wondered what happened to the time when we could shrug it off and get back to the movie and popcorn or get perspective through a sanity-check conversation with a roommate.

Being an optimist and also a realist, I had never bitten into the happily-ever-after sentiment. I knew it would require mutual effort, but it became quickly apparent that this wonderful thing called marriage would need the kind of time and attention a gardener gives her prize-winning roses. Tending to every little detail in order to revel in the beauty and enjoy the fragrant evening strolls through thick trellises never happens magically or overnight. Creating that kind of beauty takes vision, daily attention, patience, wisdom, and tenacious resolve; qualities we had obviously not cultivated yet.

A new understanding of biblical principles we had lived as singles and taught to others was about to be taken to a much deeper level. Daily practicing the things Jesus had taught and modeled would test our mettle and grow our faith. We now had a new platform to live out what it looked like to love someone with no regard to ourselves. Applying the teachings of Jesus—such as putting others first, laying down one's life for a friend, going the second mile, turning the other cheek, forgiving seventy times seven, and first removing the log in one's own eye—took on new dynamics. But suddenly, with emotions swirling, dying to self, living authentically, and loving unconditionally felt like doing the high jump while standing flat footed.

One of mankind's deepest longings is to be known and loved. Because of that, some of our biggest fears revolve around being known and *not* loved. By God's design, we were getting to know each other deeply and on many levels. While our journey toward intimacy and being fully known was exciting and the process necessary, we were discovering that what we had promised at the altar would literally take an act of God to carry out.

"For better or for worse." Those words took on new meaning throughout our first year. It was harder than we had estimated. This was work. The rubber had met the road. We found ourselves in a holy crucible called marriage. There were now glimpses its real work had begun. But would we stay the course long enough to see its intended results?

And I am certain that God, who began the good work within you, will continue his work until it is finally finished on the day when Christ Jesus returns.
—Philippians 1:6

chapter 11

Chicken and Dumplings Redemption

I remember our first real, documentable argument. It came about four months after our wedding. I knew Norm had always loved his mother's homemade chicken and dumplings with tomatoes. She had made them for lunch a couple times when I visited his family. She always served them with his favorite kind of corn bread, and of course for dessert there was lemon meringue pie. It was football season, and I decided I would surprise him with his favorite boyhood meal. At halftime I peeked into the den and told him lunch was ready.

The morning hours had melted away as my labor of love came together. The pie was exactly like I had hoped, with golden-brown merengue peaks spaced evenly over the top. The tomatoes were chilled and ready, and the corn bread smelled and even looked just like his mother's. I had cooked and deboned the chicken, made the dough from scratch, and rolled it out while the seasoned soup bubbled in the pot.

As I cut each piece of dough and dropped it into the creamy broth, how was I to know his mother had always rolled and carefully hand-stretched each dumpling square until it was so paper thin you could see right through it? My mother had always made them nice and thick. Chewy and substantial, just how I liked them. The kitchen was a floury mess from my efforts, and the whole house bragged that wonderful chicken and crusty corn bread aroma. This would be my own personal one-handed touchdown. I might deserve a jubilant chicken dance celebration in the in zone.

Walking into the little dining room after I had beckoned my husband from his lazy day of football, he slid into in his usual place at the table and I into mine. Table properly set, lemon pie serving as the centerpiece, and plates steaming in front of us, flanked by corn bread, butter, and of course sweet southern iced tea, I was ready for the big moment.

Norm sipped his tea. Like a king at his banquet, he seemed pleased enough by the table spread before him. Then with me refusing to eat before he had sampled the main course, he chowed down. After sampling a couple of bites of his chicken and dumplings, with me anxiously awaiting the verdict, he continued to chew for what seemed like a longer-than-usual amount of time. Then without warning, he slowly placed his napkin back onto the table, got up, and made his way back to the football game. He just disappeared. I could still hear the play-by-play blaring in the den.

Now I know that a reaction is different from a response. But what ensued as I quickly followed his steps down the hallway might better be left to the imagination. Whether you define it as a response or a reaction, this one included weeping, wailing, and some gnashing of teeth. I would mainly be the one weeping and wailing, while Norm sat passively on the loveseat, gnashing his teeth.

What he heard was a crystal-clear rehearsal of my every dumpling-making effort. "I have slaved away in that kitchen for hours with the sweat dripping from my face and down my back."

What I heard was Norm's measured but staunch explanation. "Those were not even remotely like my Mother's dumplings." That was something I had already surmised without the extra nine words.

Although I eventually learned how to make chicken and dumplings, which Norm (and later our kids) couldn't get enough of, that first food fight was actually an icebreaker. That explosion seemed to invite other painful disagreements and reactions. Disappointment popped up everywhere. We were not yellers, so our disagreements had always been civil, even measured. We had learned the art of disagreeing without words. But there were days you could cut the tension in the room with a knife. Often without a lot of volume, we made our points in other ways.

Like with the dumpling episode, Norm's go-to method of handling conflict was to say nothing and exit the room like greased lightning. He seemed to run from all appearance of controversy, usually before the emotion in the air had time to materialize into words. I think he could smell a disagreement from a distance.

My tendency when there was discord was to ask Norm not to walk away and press him to talk it through to resolution. I was the take the bull by the horns kind of girl, so I insisted he stay and stand his ground in the midst of the emotion. I knew all too well what happened when there was no resolution over time.

Though my parents' story could fill a book and is now a beautiful picture of the redemptive power and goodness of God, it wasn't so when I was growing up. During my childhood and for decades, my parents' relationship was fraught with turmoil. Loud, unending arguments were common. Their quarrels grew more painful as time went on, often escalating to someone leaving the house. Year-after-year tensions remained thick creating a sense of hopelessness. The four of us kids learned our own set of coping skills out of necessity. Being the oldest and the self-appointed peacemaker for the family, I served as the go-between for as long as I can remember.

I would plead Mother's case to Daddy and vice versa until there was a workable, though less than effective, solution. I had known even then that my helping them come to a compromise just to have some momentary peace was only a Band-Aid over a gaping wound. Undoubtedly, there had been rivers that led to their own sea of pain. Through all those years of listening carefully and thinking on my feet to plead someone else's case, I got pretty good at articulating clearly and succinctly what someone without words was trying to say. I learned to stand in the gap and fight. I became adept at painting verbal pictures for the sake of peace, and succinctly speaking truth in love.

I might have made a decent lawyer had I not had my mind made up otherwise from a young age.

"What do you want to be when you grow up?" asked my fourth-grade friend as we played school out on the carport.

"I want to be a teacher, and a mommy. Now, please take your seat and raise your hand if you have any more questions," I instructed as I returned to grading her make-believe spelling test using lots of red ink.

Beginning in my college years, God began the redemptive process of healing the wounds I carried. That process is ongoing. Perhaps because of my childhood, or because we all long for heaven, it became my mission to create atmospheres in which God's love and peace were evident. I wanted wherever I called home to be one of those little pieces of heaven. That desire in itself was born for good reason, but can easily cross over into the desire to control for the sake of peace.

On the other hand, in all his growing up years, Norm had never seen his parents argue. Yes, really. His recollection is that there were few words exchanged at all. He describes his life growing up as peaceful and loving but skimming across the surface. Though serene, there had been little depth of communication in his home. Norm had a huge blank space when it came to the topics of connecting deeply and handling conflict. One by one the differences emerged. Instead of driving us to depend more on Jesus, they served to create a creeping distance.

Though we were crazy about each other and would quickly kiss and make up after conflict, we often behaved like two ticks with no dog. Though we both had given our lives to Christ and had asked Him to grow us into His likeness, we were two strong, blind newlyweds unknowingly trying to get our deepest needs met from each other. What an effort in total futility! All too often we lived our lives as though the other person could fill us up and meet our gaping needs for love, appreciation, and self-worth. More often than we wanted to admit, we found ourselves angry and disillusioned.

Yes, of course we knew in our heads that a relationship with God was the only road to life. Intellectually we could tell you that only

Christ could meet our deepest needs. But now, in the serious business of our marriage, it became a much more difficult matter altogether to apply that knowledge to our own hearts in the heat of the moment or when raw emotions were swirling.

In an attempt to explain the meaning of the gospel of Christ, a pastor named Jack Miller once said: "Cheer up: You're a worse sinner than you ever dared imagine, and you're more loved than you ever dared hope." He explained that each of us wakes up every morning, desperately needing a Savior. The first couple years of our lives together we realize we didn't really get that. At least not enough to let it transform our responses under pressure and permeate our hearts enough to let it make the difference.

At Christmas, finances were so tight we didn't think we would have enough to cover our rent. We prayed for God to provide as we trimmed our already tight budget.

Our house had one of those little mailboxes where the postal carrier drops your mail into the slot from your porch and you open it from inside your living room. We were leaving for our Christmas break and had been praying for several weeks that God would somehow supply the money we owed for rent. Just as we were going out the door, Norm asked me to check the drop box one more time. As I opened the little wooden door with a small crystal pull, there in an envelope was a check. It was for a little over $700. We had forgotten about a reimbursement we were due, but it was just enough to pay our rent. God had supplied that need from a source we had not even remembered to pray about.

There were other unexpected gifts during that difficult year, like the day we discovered grocery bags full of food anonymously left on our porch in February when our cabinets and fridge were almost empty for the weeks ahead. Another came when Norm was given the opportunity to pick up extra part-time work with a landscape company called Lawn Rangers. That job later grew into a full-time position.

Through each trial and frustration, we were learning more of what it looked like to trust God in all circumstances. At the same time, we were experiencing our total inability to love each other as we had promised. The feelings of love proved fickle as we bumped up against the work and choices involved in having the kind of marriage we had pictured before we said our vows. What was love actually? A noun? A verb? An illusive dream?

Love is patient and kind. Love is not jealous or boastful or proud or rude. It does not demand its own way. It is not irritable, and it keeps no record of being wronged. It does not rejoice about injustice but rejoices whenever the truth wins out. Love never gives up, never loses faith, is always hopeful, and endures through every circumstance. When I was a child, I spoke and thought and reasoned as a child. But when I grew up, I put away childish things. Now we see things imperfectly, like puzzling reflections in a mirror, but then we will see everything with perfect clarity. All that I know now is partial and incomplete, but then I will know everything completely, just as God now knows me completely.

Three things will last forever—faith, hope, and love—and the greatest of these is love.

—1 Corinthians 13:4–7, 11–13

chapter 12

The Pivot on the Porch

It was early spring, not even a year after we had exchanged our vows and set off in married bliss. We both knew there was no such thing as a perfect marriage and we had even expected to have some ups and downs. But as we surveyed the current state of affairs, we both knew something had to change.

With finances in disarray, frustrations and disagreements became more common than we ever anticipated. Each other's weaknesses all too often took center stage. We both realized we needed another set of eyes and ears if we were ever going to move to a better place in our marriage.

Our pastor, Harold Bullock, came to our home in Fort Worth at our request. Besides being our church's founding pastor, he had the gift of wisdom and was a sought-after counselor and teacher. His eyes and ears were tuned to the Father's heart and we trusted him to shoot straight with us.

Norm and I shared with him the most pressing issues in our marriage as we saw them. After listening, clarifying and summarizing, he helped each of us get some much-needed perspective. He shared some Biblical principles he and his wife had learned about how to love each other sacrificially and the fact that we all fall short of the standard; loving as Jesus loved. Assuring us what we wanted was impossible apart from Christ working in us, he prayed for us. At the same time, with compassion and wisdom, he seemed to have confidence that we would figure it out because we both knew Jesus and walked with Him tenaciously. That seemed the most hopeful piece.

As he readied to leave, Harold asked if he could speak with me privately, so he and I stepped out on the front porch. Our counselor began by saying that he believed God would use all our differences and financial pressures to grow us. He stressed again that one of the main purposes of marriage was to refine us and shape us into the image of Christ. His words breathed life and hope. When all this was done, I would look more like Jesus.

Then he got straight to the reason for the private counseling session, "Denise, you are going to have to let your husband learn to lead," he said frankly speaking the hard truth in love. "Norm, like most men, doesn't know how to be the leader he wants to be, especially when it comes to marriage. Women are more often the natural leaders. But many times men have to be given time and opportunity to fail in order to learn to lead well." He paused as I chewed on what he was saying.

"Letting him lead will mean releasing the reins of control. Because you are more comfortable leading, your tendency will be to hold the reigns tightly and at any cost. Letting go might be one of the hardest things you've ever done. Norm will probably fail a few times along the way. And I hate to tell you this," he paused, "you may need to be willing to go down with the ship, singing 'Nearer my God to Thee.' And you may have to do it over and over again," he said, with a hint of humor and sympathy in his voice.

He smiled only slightly as the seriousness of his words lingered in the air before he continued. Absorbing his admonishment like a sponge, I was beginning to understand the gravity and weight of the counsel Harold offered. "Of course, you have a choice," he concluded. "But if you don't let go of the reins of your marriage, you'll wind up in a few years with a forty-year-old boy for a husband."

He may have said more before he walked to his car, but I heard nothing else. Those sobering words hit their mark with stealth precision. I feel sure my inner defense attorney wanted to fly into action to list for him all my credentials as well as Norm's shortcomings. But by God's grace I stood silent; pondering his guidance, just letting it seep deeper into bone and marrow.

Those were indeed some of the wisest words ever spoken to this young teacher, dreamer, perfectionist, and newlywed. I longed for a God-centered marriage. Norm and I each desired our relationship to reflect that picture of Christ and the church we had cemented in our minds on our wedding day. But, like every couple I've ever known, having that picture take life and become a reality was going to require much more than we could have possibly envisioned then.

By the grace and mercy of a faithful God, I heard and determined on our front porch to take our counselor's wise advice to heart. Respecting and knowing Harold as I did, I knew he had spoken God's words to my ears, and I let them sink deep into my discouraged heart. Heeding his counsel to let go of the reins wouldn't come without moments of pain and a measure of sacrifice.

Control was something I was unknowingly quite good at. I had learned to embrace the power of those reins without even knowing it. Looking back, I realize I had wrestled with fear-based control and an overly sensitive, critical spirit pretty much daily … and twice on Sundays, especially when our ship was indeed going down with me standing on its deck. Standing there with my voice quivering from both fear and anger, I remembered sometimes hearing Harold's counsel to let go and let Norm learn to lead while I sang that song for yet another time. I confess, I usually didn't feel the "Nearer My God to Thee" part, certainly not as our ship took on water and my anger boiled.

Looking back, there were days that frustration, disillusionment, and the desire to pack it up and go home raged like a hurricane for control of my mind. In the years that followed, there were times when it almost seemed appropriate to put my hand over my heart as I visualized the waters crashing onto the deck of our ship.

I shared Harold's counsel to us with a friend, Sabra, who was also my small group leader. She reminded me of a Bible study through the book of Ephesians she and I had done together. I had learned from our study that a man's number one need was for respect, especially from his wife. We discussed some of the ways wives sometimes show disrespect and dishonor to their husbands. That conversation was long and gave me new awareness of my own sin.

Ephesians was a book I knew well. In chapter 5, the apostle Paul talks about how we are to submit to one another out of reverence for Christ. He then breaks down all the various relationships that existed in his day and gives each group specific instructions. I remember thinking that the husband had been given the most difficult task of them all. Norm was being instructed to love me, give up his rights, and lay down his life for me like Jesus had done for His bride, the church. Husbands were being called to imitate sacrificial love with the cross of Christ as their standard.

Over the next few weeks, God revealed to me several areas in which I had been responding to Norm with an attitude that spoke the exact opposite of honor. I realized that I nobly thought Norm should have to earn my respect before I gave it. And of course, I had set myself as the best choice for both judge and jury in that department.

A vivid picture of what giving my respect might look like came to mind. A couple months earlier, Norm and I had attended a relationship seminar on the gift of honor. The keynote speaker, Gary Smalley, who later wrote a book on the topic, shared an illustration that I have never forgotten.

All weekend, he and his wife recounted the miraculous story of how God helped them put their broken marriage back together during a time they teetered on the brink of divorce. Using a sparkling cubic zirconia which he pulled from his coat pocket and dangled before us on a chain, he relayed the story of how God had shown him through prayer and his study of scripture that his wife was worth far more than the most priceless diamonds.

Time and again he was reminded of the truth that his wife had been created in the very image of God. Treating her as such would change everything. Our speaker shared how he had made a choice to daily focus only on her worth. Thus, he carried that diamond in his pocket as a reminder. By transferring the beauty, value, and brilliance of diamonds to his wife, his feelings and actions began to change. The part that struck me most was how by leading out in faith, his heart was transformed to the point that each time he saw his wife enter a room he said, "She literally took my breath away."

By agreeing with God about his wife's intrinsic value and treating her with honor, he watched as God softened her heart as well. In time they began making steps toward each other. Soon there was godly sorrow over sin, followed by true repentance. They sought forgiveness from each other for the many ways they had each contributed to pain and the dark place in which they had found themselves.

Over time God restored their marriage, giving them back their first love and the oneness that had been intended. The ripple effects of their reconciliation reached into the lives of their children, grandchildren, church, and far beyond their family.

Remembering their story drew me to see the parallels of what I needed to do regarding honor. So as a way of letting go of my tendency to control, I made the decision to give Norm my respect as someone gives her lover an extravagant gift. Like our speaker who envisioned diamonds, my gift would be elegantly wrapped in love and would be the daily choice of speaking and responding with honor to the man of my dreams. My gift would be without contingencies, not based on Norm's response. I knew it had to be a choice, not a feeling; an act of obedience and an act of faith and trust in God alone to transform my heart. I chose to leave the long-term results of that decision to God.

Expressing respect for Norm took on a life of its own after that. Choosing to let my words be seasoned with love, kindness, and curiosity instead of judgment and fault-finding became true desires of my heart. Sometimes my attempts were feeble. There were days when failure and discouragement surrounded me in their attempt to derail my resolve. But there were other days when rays of hope broke through in the heat of an emotional conversation, seeing God give me the grace to remain silent when what was on the tip of my tongue would have been destructive.

I was encouraged by studying the way Jesus treated people. I read through the book of Proverbs which has thirty-one chapters by reading a chapter a day. Month after month I read, asking God for practical ways to apply the wisdom dripping from every page. Each time I read, I mined new treasures and fresh insights. By steeping myself in Proverbs, I was reminded of the power I held as a woman to either build up or tear down my own "house" with my words and actions. I knew it was true. My eyes and tone often held the power of life and death in our relationship. The principles of the Bible helped guide, admonish, and inspire me as I began the difficult task of creating new habits and laying down old ones.

Catching glimpses of God's pleasure over that decision and its myriad expressions has been for me an inexpressible, private joy that has spurred me on when the feelings often would not come. It was like I was being pursued by the Hound of Heaven, who whispered much-needed encouragement over that central and obviously crucial arena of my life and our marriage. That same Hound of Heaven is the true and eternal Lover of my soul.

And can you guess? As those difficult—yes, sometimes downright impossible—choices yielded sincere desire and emotion, both Norm and I saw our love and respect for each other grow exponentially. We learned that when you make the right choices often enough, the passion will follow later. We learned early on that feelings are fickle friends and make for an inaccurate measuring stick.

As the years became decades, that decision toward respect and honor, along with many sincere prayers for my husband's growth, wisdom, and maturity in leadership, changed us both in ways and through circumstances too numerous to list in this chapter.

I stand in awe of God's tenacious mercy and of how He has wisely and gently grown us both in the whole love and respect arena of our marriage. Norm, who will admit he had only a vague idea of how to lead at first, has become an amazing leader. His leadership, though, is wonderfully seasoned with wisdom, patience, grace, kindness, and thankfully large amounts of humor. And over the years I have been able to reap the unspoken, priceless rewards of laying down my honed and often ready weapons of tongue and attitude in obedience to a faithful God who rewards closet prayers and sees those countless split-second faith choices.

That day on the porch, I made a deliberate pivot in the hard direction of releasing the reins of my marriage along with my natural bent toward control. It was only a small step, a simple decision to let go and let God have an entrenched place in my heart. He instead would take the reins. Deep down I knew that offering it up to Him in simple surrender was the only way forward.

There were no violins or choral singers over my choice to make a turn that day, but there may have been angels rejoicing. And I believe God's pleasure surrounded our little porch altar as He showed me my need for change and as I breathed a prayer for help.

I still look back with an amazed and grateful heart to that pivotal, life-changing decision made during a teary, private conversation between a wise pastor and a disillusioned young bride on a Texas porch.

As the Scriptures say, "A man leaves his father and mother and is joined to his wife, and the two are united into one." This is a great mystery, but it is an illustration of the way Christ and the church are one. So again I say, each man must love his wife as he loves himself, and the wife must respect her husband.

—Ephesians 5:31–33

chapter 13

Strength under Control

Note: This story is from my childhood. I know it doesn't fit the timeline, but it illustrates how God teaches us spiritual concepts through things He made if we're listening. God taught me about gentleness, which is actually strength under control, through my horse. I wanted to include it here for you.

I will never forget the day my daddy told us we were going to pick out our horse. Excitedly, we all climbed into Daddy's Jeep, and after what seemed like forever, our drive to Lincolnton, North Carolina, ended at a beautiful horse farm bordered by a white rail fence that seemed to stretch on for miles. It was a brilliant, sunny day, and I could see the horse trailers, which had just arrived from California, parked beside the red-and-white barn. You could hear the snorts, whinnies, and neighs of road-weary, spirited, young horses inside as we waited with anticipation alongside other eager buyers.

As the horses were carefully backed out of their trailers one by one and led to the sale barn, my mother, younger brother, and I looked on from an acceptable distance. While Daddy and all the other buyers carefully sized up each unique horse, it seemed clear that no one wanted to seem too impressed over any one choice. It was a poker table they had come to that day; and every prize was grand.

Daddy was one of the first to size up, declare, and purchase his horse. The three of us were almost gleeful as we watched him lead in our direction a beautiful golden palomino, with platinum tail and mane. His white blaze matched his stocking hooves. Daddy had chosen a proud, fancy kind of horse. I had remembered seeing them in the Rose Bowl Parade. I had never seen an animal so magnificent at the time, and very seldom since, for that matter.

The trip home was full of happy anticipation and talk of how the contents of the horse trailer behind us would change our lives. Actually, I loved all my new responsibilities down at the barn. My jobs included currying, feeding, cleaning stalls, and keeping the watering trough full. I especially loved riding him to the creek and washing him down. I quickly became a pro at offering him broken carrots from an open hand without getting my fingers nibbled off.

His name was soon declared Nugget. Daddy worked with him for months to break him in. Nugget learned quickly. Shortly we realized his senses were keen, and he could smell fear, pleasure, and the barn a mile away. Daddy had been raised with work horses and was a natural at teaching them to behave and respect the process. He trained Nugget in the slow and fast gaits of his breed. I became an avid student of all things horse and learned to ride and train him right along with my parents and brother.

A five-gaited racking horse, Nugget was highly spirited and fast moving for my daddy but as gentle as a lamb when a child was placed on his back. My mother quickly learned how to ride and show him. Over time Nugget became a grand show horse who was a thrill and pleasure to watch both from the fields and trails of our family farm as well as from the sawdust-laden show arenas where we spent many a weekend. Blue ribbons and scrapbooks full of newspaper clippings decorated our kitchen table. Entering and competing at area and regional horse shows became a favorite family pastime.

Our daily treks down to the creek, often riding bareback and holding only tufts of white, wiry mane, became times of quiet reflection that gave me a serene place to debrief. I always loved just being blissfully alone at the creek or on a trail with Nugget and God.

Many lessons are learned from animals and nature. But the lesson I caught while watching how over time a wild, unbroken, undisciplined horse becomes a trained, gentled, trusted friend yielded life lessons of process, patience, and strength under control that have had far-reaching application for me over the years.

One of my most vivid memories of him, is of the day we brought Nugget to our little mill village house to give him a bath and perhaps to show him off just a little. I was pretty sure no one in our neighborhood had a grand show horse like ours.

With our pails of warm water drawn and hose at the ready in our little gravel driveway, my brother and I stood equipped and eager for action. Daddy always "parked" Nugget with his front feet stretched out like he was trained to do at the end of his horse shows while we scrubbed and washed his golden palomino coat and white mane until it glistened. We were all enjoying the soaking-wet moment when something spooked Nugget. He came out of his pose, twirled around, and reared up. Suddenly he pulled free from the relaxed hold on the rope my mother held just a second before.

Off he bolted up the quiet gravel road in front of our house, tail high, ears back in excitement. First, he did a trot; then, breaking into a fast gait, he headed toward the main road and the possibility of oncoming traffic. We all yelled for him to stop, and Daddy chased him futilely for a distance. As fast as lightning, he was out of sight in no time.

Jumping into our Jeep with horse trailer in tow, we pulled out of the driveway, and drove off in the direction we had seen him galloping away.

When we finally caught sight of him, he was full speed ahead down the main road we had hoped he wouldn't reach. There were a few oncoming cars, but because it was a rural farming area, they managed to slow as he approached. They seemed to be enjoying the spectacle as it's not every day you can watch a show horse prancing down the road. Thankfully, he eventually took a turn off the main road and headed across a garden or two and through a schoolyard. He ended up in an enormous, grassy field. The green backdrop seemed to go on over hill and dale forever.

He was a beautiful sight to behold as the bright sun shimmered off his golden coat and flowing mane and tail as he pranced and performed, free and proud against an artist's palette of green that summer afternoon. It almost seemed an interruption of something majestic and holy when Daddy and some other men who had come to help finally cornered him and brought him to a halt. Nugget, lathered and scared, seemed more than grateful for the companionship as the men patted him down and loaded him with care into the horse trailer for his trip back to the barn.

He was our first horse. He will always hold a special place in our family's hearts. Our Nugget eventually became Old Nugget. He was such a pleasure to our entire family as well as others who saw him "dance" and show his stuff for years. He never lost his mighty spirit, and he never ceased to be gentle as well. He just seemed to know when each was appropriate.

For ever since the world was created, people have seen the earth and sky. Through everything God made, they can clearly see his invisible qualities–his eternal power and divine nature. So they have no excuse for not knowing God.
–Romans 1:20

chapter14

Slaying Dragons

God was using our marriage to change our hearts. After meeting with Harold we had a better understanding of our own contributions to the tone our marriage had acquired. The work had only just begun. Acknowledging key areas that needed work seemed a start in itself and gave us hope. Now we needed to begin slaying some of the dragons that threatened to eat our lunch.

A gift we could never have afforded ourselves as newlyweds came when someone in our church anonymously paid for us to attend a weekend marriage retreat. Never underestimate the power of the gift of a meaningful experience.

The flyer said it was "a weekend of discovery ... a lifetime of love," designed for couples desiring to improve and deepen their relationship. It said we could learn to communicate better and connect on a deeper level. Was it that obvious that we needed both? Though we had no clue as to what was coming, we were grateful to have the chance to get away and grow. Truth be known, we were both a bit skeptical and maybe a little cynical as to the actual value of weekend retreats to change ingrained patterns and help us make significant course corrections. We were wrong.

Through the course of the weekend, we realized just how desperately we needed to lighten up and take ourselves less seriously. Attending the retreat with us were friends from our church who were probably the funniest two people on earth. Through them, I witnessed the value of humor in working through serious issues. It seemed that being able to laugh acted as a lubricant for most any sticky situation.

Solomon taught that laughter from a joyful heart is good medicine. More than Norm, I needed the big dose. It had been a while since I could remember feeling joyful and light-hearted about much of anything. That weekend we found ourselves in need of a little help in the hilarity department. So, God sent the cavalry. Their names were Rusty and Becky. Norm and Rusty played off each other's jokes all weekend, while Becky and I served as the sensible ones who giggled at more appropriate times and kept the boys out of trouble. Just one glance in their direction was usually all it took. As the weekend continued, the medicine took effect.

The conference leaders, a couple who had sat where we were at one time, spoke with empathy and clarity about the value of each session. They shared their journey of how God had healed their marriage, and were transparent about their struggles along the way.

Our first assignment had specific instructions. We were to leave our meeting center in silence, walk back to our rooms without a word, and study an inventory of terms we had been given for use in answering questions and expanding conversation over the course of the weekend. Our list contained about one hundred different emotions and adjectives for expressing our feelings. It included choices such as *spontaneous, whimsical, indignant, pensive, elated, suspicious, constructive* ... You get the picture.

Back in our room, Norm and I studied the word list with great resolve. When our time of silence ended, I sat ready for a plethora of fresh-off-the-presses terminology hurling me blissfully into territory yet unknown to womankind. Norm looked across the room from his perch on the bed, holding his list and looking like he had just pulled his hand out of the cookie jar. Somehow sensing my lofty expectations for depth and meaningful conversation, he quickly confessed, "Honey, honestly, about the only words I could relate to here were *happy, sad,* and *hungry.*" I realized the blissful new heights would have to wait. We discovered Norm was not alone among the men who attended the retreat. Their universal lack of words and common desire for creative ways to communicate with their wives became a bonding agent for them.

A portion of the weekend had been designed to allow us time and resources to reflect on the beauty and complementary nature of our differences. One session focused on God's creative glory in how men and women were designed to uniquely reflect different parts of the divine nature. Norm and I began to appreciate our opposite personalities as unique ways to mirror God's image. By focusing on God's purposes in our differences, we were handed a new lens through which to view each other.

With each activity, God gave us reminders of the reasons we had fallen in love in the first place. He helped us to understand that we had something special, something only God could give us: hope combined with a mutual commitment.

A key for me was acknowledging that Norm was not my enemy. We made the mutual decision to fight for our marriage instead of with each other. We were taught the principles of clearing up offenses quickly and cherishing and protecting our relationship as the priority and primary one above all others except for our personal relationships with God. And I was reminded of the importance of praying for each other's growth in areas of strength as well as areas of weakness.

The retreat leaders shared a vision of how our marriage relationship would lay the foundation for our children and would leave a legacy for generations to come. That broadened our perspective and made us realize there was more at stake than just our often self-centered happiness.

With each valuable session, my initial attitude of cynicism glared at me. I realized the value of getting away by ourselves for the purpose of deepening our marriage even for a weekend. We got the very real sense that weekends like that were actually a wise, worthwhile investment in our future. We would need a tune-up now and then.

For three days we learned new concepts and were afforded time and space to reflect on our marriage in a way we couldn't have done in the flow of everyday life. It was like taking time to sharpen our saw.

That weekend I began to see how my own pride had undermined my dreams and had contributed to many of our frustrations and places of impasse. As I repented, I felt my heart soften and was surprised to see Norm move toward me. Again I was reminded that the only person I could change was myself through the power of the cross. Trying either consciously or subconsciously to change Norm was only a way to drive a wedge.

As the weekend progressed, couples opened up over meals as we realized familiar threads and places where we all grappled in the realms of connection and communication. Somehow in the laughter, discovery, and fun of that weekend, everyone seemed encouraged with the realization that all of us, no matter how long we had been married, struggled with many of the same basic issues. Like ice breakers, discovering common threads helped us to take down barriers and be more willing to share our journeys.

We witnessed that being real and vulnerable enough to reveal even parts of our pain can pull down some of the barriers we all put up around our hearts. I will be the first to admit that being open and letting people in didn't come easily nor quickly for me. Was it my pride, or was it that I feared being rejected if the masks were allowed to come down? Did I enjoy the mystery of anonymity so much that I would die on that hill? Sometimes, I realized, the answer was "yes."

Hearing other couples' stories and being able to laugh and cry with people who had similar pain in their eyes helped Norm and me understand we weren't alone. The experience also gave us an appreciation for our mutual commitment to embrace and put into practice whatever it took to improve our marriage. We began to see ourselves as a team pulling in the same direction.

Instead of buying into the lie that parts of our relationship were hopelessly set in motion and would never change, we began to understand that our marriage was in process. Thankfully that process would continue changing us for the rest of our lives. That weekend Norm and I wrote love letters to each other and read them out loud in the privacy of our room. Tears flowed as we renewed our vows of commitment through a marriage covenant.

It was almost a relief when I began to understand that I would most likely always have infinitely more words than Norm. I began to get the reality that he expresses his love for me most often by doing things like fixing the broken furnace, putting a bathroom where the closet was, and putting gas in my car without my knowing it. Norm is a doer, not a talker.

That weekend we made a few steps in the right direction. Discovering the riches and beauty God intended for us would take dedication, patience, and time. We were just getting started in our journey toward oneness. But that weekend supplied a dose of laughter and some useful tools for slaying a few of our dragons.

Someone had anonymously invested in us by paying our registration fee for the marriage retreat weekend. Someone whose name remained a secret had reached in and given us a valuable experience at a crucial time in our marriage. It was a love gift and a point of change for which we will always be grateful, and from which we learned the value of quietly investing in others. Whoever you are, thank you! We pray God has multiplied the investment back to you.

But when you give to someone in need, don't let your left hand know what your right hand is doing. Give your gifts in private, and your Father, who sees everything, will reward you.
                                                    —Matthew 6:3–4

chapter 15

Legacy

Harold's sermons and teaching often stressed the fact that anything we put our hopes and faith in other than Jesus will let us down and eventually destroy us. That is the story of mankind; people and nations throughout history trying to find happiness apart from God. We were learning he was right. And we wanted to learn what it looked like to put our hopes in Christ alone. Hungry and eager to grow in our faith, we became like sponges soaking up all the wisdom and counsel we could over the next couple of years. One subject that came up quite often involved legacy. What would the lasting effect or impact of our lives be? Deep down we knew it was a question worth asking.

Jesus often taught about the future and the kingdom of God. I thought it was kind of like the idea of legacy. He taught that faithfulness in the little things was necessary if a person wanted to be entrusted with more. I hoped the seed that had been sown in me would prove to be good seed that multiplied over time. I prayed God would show me more as I proved faithful with what He had already given.

In Matthew 13 Jesus tells His disciples a story. Whether in our marriage, ministry, raising children, or in my business, God seems to bring principles like this one to mind; and because His word is living and active, each time I read it I may get a new application depending on what I'm going through. I was tempted to summarize this story for you, but it's so valuable that I wanted you to read it for yourself.

The Parable of the Sower

Later that same day Jesus left the house and sat beside the lake. A large crowd soon gathered around him, so he got into a boat. Then he sat there and taught as the people stood on the shore. He told many stories in the form of parables, such as this one:

"Listen! A farmer went out to plant some seeds. As he scattered them across his field, some seeds fell on a footpath, and the birds came and ate them. Other seeds fell on shallow soil with underlying rock. The seeds sprouted quickly because the soil was shallow. But the plants soon wilted under the hot sun, and since they didn't have deep roots, they died. Other seeds fell among thorns that grew up and choked out the tender plants. Still other seeds fell on fertile soil, and they produced a crop that was thirty, sixty, and even a hundred times as much as had been planted! Anyone with ears to hear should listen and understand."

His disciples came and asked him, "Why do you use parables when you talk to the people?"

He replied, "You are permitted to understand the secrets of the Kingdom of Heaven, but others are not. To those who listen to my teaching, more understanding will be given, and they will have an abundance of knowledge. But for those who are not listening, even what little understanding they have will be taken away from them. That is why I use these parables.

For they look, but they don't really see, they hear, but they don't really listen or understand …

"Now listen to the explanation of the parable about the farmer planting seeds: The seed that fell on the footpath represents those who hear the message about the Kingdom and don't understand it. Then the evil one comes and snatches away the seed that was planted in their hearts. The seed on the rocky soil represents those who hear the message and immediately receive it with joy. But since they don't have deep roots, they don't last long. They fall away as soon as they have problems or are persecuted for believing God's word. The seed that fell among the thorns represents those who hear God's word, but all too quickly the message is crowded out by the worries of this life and the lure of wealth, so no fruit is produced. The seed that fell on good soil represents those who truly hear and understand God's word and produce a harvest of thirty, sixty, or even a hundred times as much as had been planted!" (Mathew 13:1–13, 18–23)

It's such a simple, yet powerful story.

Norm and I wanted our lives to matter. We began to pray that the good seed God had planted in our marriage and in our hearts as individuals would take hold and yield a harvest. Whether that was thirty, sixty, or a hundredfold was up to Him. We wanted to be faithful to whatever He called us to. We prayed He would multiply our love for each other into the lives of people.

Since we had chosen to join Hope, a church whose central focus was making disciples, it came as no surprise that we would be challenged to grow in our faith and get out of our comfort zones. The values at Hope were lived out mainly through the home groups. These were small groups of men or women, in which we shared life, studied the Bible, reached out to our communities, and prayed for each other.

Small groups made a life-changing impact on our lives. We threw fun parties or showers for those getting married or having babies. There always seemed to be a steady stream of food, songs, hilarious skits, and a plethora of gifts for the grateful honorees. Whenever there was a known need in the community, our groups responded in practical ways. Our members painted houses, cooked meals, provided auto repair, raked leaves, and delivered groceries. We thrived on service and being attentive to others' needs. Hope was a church that sought to be the loving hands and feet of Jesus to our city.

Within the context of a spiritual community, there was ample opportunity for us to give and receive training, counsel, encouragement, accountability, and perspective as well as just have hilarious fun together. Many strong leaders with vision poured themselves into our lives during those years. Our home group leaders, Craig and Sabra, mentored us for a few years and became lifelong friends. They were instrumental in helping us stretch our faith, memorize the Bible, and apply the principles we learned from our Bible studies. Their servant's hearts and vibrant enthusiasm for the gospel painted an indelible picture of how to give your life away in Christ's name.

To help us get clarity about our legacy, Craig and Sabra gave us a challenge. Reminding us of the passage in Proverbs that talks about people with no vision failing at life, they asked us to pretend we were eighty years old and sitting in rocking chairs on the front porch of our home, reminiscing about our lives. They asked us to write down what we wanted our lives to look like from our make-believe elderly perspective. We were to look deep into our hearts and envision our dreams—not just to dream, but to pray and ask what God wanted to do with us if He granted us those years and the opportunity to look back over them someday. It was an assignment we took seriously.

So over the next couple of weeks, we prayed, dreamed, and wrote. That exercise was a sobering realization that we could have a part in creating the kind of legacy we would leave. Though we knew God had a plan for our lives and that He alone knew our future, we were challenged to tap into the desires God had already planted in us and to put those core convictions in writing.

With seriousness and excitement, we dreamed out loud, brainstormed together, and scribbled it all down. Until that moment, we hadn't unearthed many of the specifics buried deep in our hearts. The exercise uncovered stirrings we had not voiced before. I can't remember everything we wrote, since we lost those notes in one of our moves. I recall I began my list with my desire to always be a teacher, multiply my life by setting yearly mentoring goals, and to be an encourager. We made a commitment to stay curious and become lifelong learners.

That exercise brought one big thing right out in the open. Both of us had a hearts' desire to have a house full of children. I remember writing down that if God someday blessed us with children, we wanted to raise them to know and love Him with their whole hearts and to love others well. We detailed our dream to create a home our children loved being in and one in which their friends would want to come over just to hang out. We joked about how someday our grown kids and grandchildren would want to sit with us in the rocking chairs on our make-believe porch.

One secret dream I remember jotting down seemed self-absorbed at the time; *Someday I want to live surrounded by water and mountains.* Something about being in that kind of beauty usually made me cry. Those were the places that best urged my soul toward quiet and drew me to be still; to worship. Someone once told me that when there were tears, I would know I had hit the real treasure. I no longer believe it indulgent to wish for such things.

Though we dreamed about Norm someday having a twelve-string, traveling the world, and the houses we'd build, it became clear that most of our dreams and goals revolved around our relationship with God, investing in people, and raising a family.

After all the back and forth of our assignment, we summed up our thoughts in one sentence: *By God's grace we want to live, laugh, love, learn, and leave a legacy.*

That simple exercise of writing down specific convictions and setting goals has proved helpful over the years. Brainstorming together in our first year of marriage served to ground us to what was important and make us aware of the brevity of life. The bottom-line takeaway from it all was our mutual desire to know and love God and to make our lives count for building His kingdom here on earth. Without realizing it then, that assignment gave us a starting point from which to launch, and a mutually-decided end goal as we began our lives together.

At the same time, we held those dreams loosely. God alone knew the chapters of our lives. As we prayed over that exercise, we were reminded that we weren't in charge.

As you might have guessed, many of those specifics didn't materialize, and nothing was exactly as we had envisioned, though some were pretty close. Amazingly, most of our core values and desires remain the same decades later. When I look back, I see that our working together to verbalize what we wanted our lives to look like has served to show us that we cannot out-dream God. We see how God worked out much of what He had put in us in ways we could never have fathomed. Using our lists as starting points, we have seen God do immeasurably more than we could have dreamed in our twenties.

It would seem that Our Lord finds our desires not too strong, but too weak. We are half-hearted creatures, fooling about with drink and sex and ambition when infinite joy is offered us, like an ignorant child who wants to go on making mud pies in a slum because he cannot imagine what is meant by the offer of a holiday at the sea. We are far too easily pleased.
—C. S. Lewis, *The Weight of Glory and Other Addresses*

chapter16

Houston

In *A Tale of Two Cities*, Charles Dickens penned words that have become perhaps the most famous opening lines in English literature. "It was the best of times, it was the worst of times, it was the age of wisdom, it was the age of foolishness." Those words are famous not only because they are true of the turmoil of eighteenth-century London and Paris during the French Revolution, but because they apply in smaller ways to all of our lives. Dickens's words rang true for us with every move.

A couple months before our first anniversary, we received two phone calls that changed our course. The first was from Mrs. Kendall. She called to say she would be moving back to her home in a few weeks, which meant we would need to find somewhere else to live.

The other call was from one of Norm's professors. With one final required field assignment in order to complete his graduate degree, he was expecting the call. Being well aware of Norm's heart for pastoring and helping plant churches, he had called to present two opportunities. Each would involve church planting. Both required a move and someone willing to relocate permanently to continue as pastor of the new work. The first request was from a church in Redlands, California. The other was from a church in Houston. Each pastor painted a picture of his church's vision and their commitment to provide housing, income, and support for the assignment. Each wanted a quick decision.

After a couple days of prayer, seeking counsel, and talking further with the pastors to find out as many details as possible about what each situation entailed, we made a decision to move to Houston. So with all our earthly possessions loaded into a small U-Haul, we said goodbye to our amazing life in Fort Worth. All Norm's vision, field training, and education was now about to be put to use.

Charles Dickens' words certainly rang true for us in Houston. With all we encountered, it became an experience God used to bring us closer to each other as we struggled through those months far from anything or anyone familiar or remotely supportive. A wise friend once told me that learning what you *don't* want to do is a valuable part of discovering what you *do* want to do. Houston became such a school for us.

It quickly became obvious that many of the church members were not on board with our mission. Almost nothing had been done in preparation for our arrival, including where we would live. We found ourselves feeling our way around from the start and at the mercy of those in charge. We were grateful for an older couple who took us under their wing and helped guide us when they saw the confusion surrounding our arrival.

At our first meeting with leaders, there appeared to be no common vision for the proposed church plant described to us over the phone a few weeks earlier. We caught on pretty quickly that some influential, vocal church members objected to our being there at all. Either the members had not understood our mission, or they saw no need for planting new churches and had made that point loud and clear. We met with definite opposition from the beginning.

Circumstances too numerous to recount enrolled us in senior-level life classes that gave us unexpected lessons that would grow us quickly and sharpen our ability to hear and heed God's voice in the future. We fought embellishments and misinformation for the duration of the summer. Norm and I found ourselves alone in Houston on an island surrounded by a sea of people, many of whom objected to our being there.

After assessing the situation, we discussed our dilemma with our contact person in Norm's graduate program. He offered us the option to leave, but encouraged us to stay and see what God would do with us in the midst of a difficult situation. He shared a few stories of how God had turned conditions like ours into a blessing in the end. We decided to stay the course.

Our first lesson was invaluable. Expectations can be deadly if you aren't willing to lay them down and walk away. Instead of working with a core group of excited people who wanted to start a church, we learned our job description was to walk door-to-door through new housing developments conducting a survey. Our assignment became to inform people of the vision for a church in their area and assess their interest level in getting involved. During the months of June, July, and August. In the Houston heat. Yes, I had become a whiner.

After just a couple of weeks, it dawned on us that our main life calling probably wouldn't involve knocking on strangers' doors for a living. I was an introvert operating in an extrovert's world out of sheer necessity. At first, it was nothing less than terrifying and painful. And hot.

I admit engaging strangers became only a little less uncomfortable as time went on. But somewhere near the middle of the summer, God mercifully gave me a love for the people behind the doors. More importantly, I got to see my man-of-few-words husband step up to the plate. He did it day after day. No complaints. None. My respect and admiration for Norm grew. My appreciation for his willingness to take the lead on my behalf in any and every circumstance went through the roof. He became my hero.

We never knew what a day might hold. Sometimes angry barking dogs or people who hated religion of any kind met us at the door. Other days half-asleep retirees told us to take a hike, skeptical housewives peered at us through a window, and unruly kids prevented any hope of a conversation. Those same days, though, were intertwined with kind homeowners welcoming us into their living rooms or greeting us from their driveways, answering our questions with kindness and candor. It was with those few that we found genuine interest and openness. Some requested we pray for them. Many opened up about heartbreaking situations. As we talked and prayed with the few, we realized that God was using us to minister to people He loved.

The possibility of creating conversations that mattered began to drive us on day after day. Almost without our knowing it, God changed our hearts as well as our perspective without doing a thing about our circumstances. We had desired our experience to be about more than just collecting data; our prayer became one of asking God to use us to show people His love and goodness. We began praying that we would become the hands and feet of Jesus that day, and that He would show us whom He wanted to love through us as we left our apartment each morning.

Our new outlook gave us energy and enthusiasm. Behind those doors were broken people just like us who woke up every morning, desperately in need of a Savior. And just like us, they needed hope for their marriages, their precious families, and hope for their future. We knew that whatever they sought could ultimately come only through a relationship with God through Christ. Our time now seemed short. With new eyes we began to see people of different cultures, socioeconomic strata, and ethnic groups—all with the same needs, fears, and desires at their core. We experienced the power of having God's perspective. It changed everything.

Focusing on God's deep love for the people behind the doors as well as our understanding of their need for the gospel became our driving force through the heat and through the fear. Norm led the way and became my example by filling out stacks of survey cards with patience and genuine enthusiasm. He always remained attentive and curious when too often I found myself complaining about being exhausted and just wanting to go back to the air-conditioning. His strength in those and other areas surfaced that summer. I got to see my husband step up to a host of unexpected plates.

We celebrated our first anniversary in Houston at Shanghai Reds. Now out of business, it was then a highly recommended spot known for their seafood and steaks. Norm had requested a table with a view of the ships coming in and out of the harbor at sunset. I decided quiet romantics are the best kind. My tears flowed that night in June as we reminisced about our tough first year's journey.

Our tradition of collecting matchbooks began at Shanghai Reds. Though neither of us smoked, we made it a habit to ask for a matchbook from every restaurant, hotel, or resort we visited and put them in a decorative jar. Then on candlelight date nights at home we would pull out the jar, pick a random matchbook, and reminisce.

God showed us His faithfulness in a thousand ways that summer. If we had left during the first difficult weeks in Houston, we would have missed them all. One special gift was finding a great apartment in a convenient location. It was there that we made great friends with whom we enjoyed burgers on the grill and game nights all summer. Two of those friends invited us on weekend trips to their hometowns of Corpus Christi and South Padre Island; places we may never have been able to visit otherwise.

Perhaps the most vivid memory we took from Houston was being there to celebrate the Fourth of July. What an amazing city with the Buffalo Bayou flowing through it! An all-American family affair with children playing freely up and down the banks of the river. In typical Texas flair, they boasted the nation's best in everything from hotdogs and apple pie to Texas brisket. Texas holds the bragging rights, if you ask me.

The entire day was filled with sights and sounds of America's founding. Smells of smoked barbecue and burgers on the grill filled the park from the host of food vendors around every corner. George and Martha Washington stopped to visit with families as they meandered through the park telling their story.

The Houston orchestra was spectacular. That evening we soaked in the light pageant over the river from our quilted perch by the river as the orchestra accompanied the brilliant fireworks exhibition with the familiar songs and marches that have bonded Americans for over two hundred years. That evening we were two in a sea of proud, grateful Americans celebrating our common heritage.

As we closed the book on our summer, we understood a little more clearly that church planting is a massive undertaking that required special gifts, vision, perseverance, and the ability to roll with unexpected punches. We also sensed that God had planted more deeply in our hearts His call for us love people wherever we go, and to be salt and light in a dark world. We wondered where those convictions would take us.

Jesus said He would build His church, and the gates of hell wouldn't prevail against it. He was talking about the church throughout history, which began in the first century. The big lesson we took from our time in Houston was that planting churches required a work of the Holy Spirit. To be successful we would need to align ourselves with His eternal purposes. Norm and I determined that entering ministry of any kind would test our mettle and stretch us out of our lofty theories and prideful, preconceived notions.

As we looked back, we realized God had been teaching us to pay attention and look hard for Him no matter the circumstances. He was also helping us embrace more fully that He is in charge and that absolutely nothing escapes His eye.

Looking at the city in our rearview mirror, we felt a little wiser and a lot less idealistic than during our starry-eyed way down that road in late May. We were also feeling a little depressed and a lot confused. Three months before, we had believed that we were most likely making a permanent move to Houston. Now on our way back to Fort Worth, we were basically homeless, jobless, and lacking any sense of direction.

After reading back over our required daily journals, Norm's professor, who had been periodically kept apprised of our situation, commended us on staying our course to see what God might do. Many of the thoughts in this chapter were recorded in daily detail for him to see and for us to recall later.

"I think you guys did well with all the challenges you faced and under the circumstances," he said.

And we know that God causes everything to work together for the good of those who love God and are called according to his purpose for them.
                                                    —*Romans 8:28*

chapter 17

Back to the Drawing Board, or Was It a Springboard?

We moved back to Fort Worth and began our search for jobs and a place to live. Grateful for a familiar rhythm, we picked up where we had left off with church and established relationships. By then it had become clear to me that I didn't like moving nearly as much as my free-spirited husband did. Yearning for a place to call home, I began praying we could just stay put for a while.

After a few weeks of living with friends, we moved into a cute apartment in a complex close to our church and not too far from my new job. You can imagine how grateful I was to have found a wonderful opportunity to teach fifth grade again. It turned out to be one of the sweetest school years ever. Did I mention I loved teaching fifth grade?

Norm began working full-time with the landscaping company he had worked for before called the Lawn Rangers. With that name there were almost daily stories around our dinner table. But they must have been pretty good at what they did because they had some large accounts with local businesses, including one keeping the south side of the Dallas/Fort Worth airport looking perfectly groomed. Beautifying homes and businesses was important, and the Lawn Rangers took it seriously. The many skills and work ethic Norm learned with that company have served him well for decades.

One of our priorities was to have people over for dinner more often that year, no matter our finances. Those simple dinners would often extend into late-night games of Pictionary, fast Uno, or spades. And because we seemed to surround ourselves with people who were so competitive, there had to be just "one more round" until they either won or were too tired to care. Good times. Great fun. Making choices to invest time in people always yields lifelong relationships and tons of memories.

Over fall break Norm and I went to Los Angeles with a church-planting team. Packing as many people, places, and experiences as possible into a week's time, it was a life-changing, vision-casting trip. On our last night there, our team joined a local church for an evening of prayer for the city. Praying over that enormous metropolis from one of the highest hills near Hollywood was an experience I will never forget. The lights of LA and all the adjoining towns sprawled out in every direction. I felt so small. It was difficult to take in. The God of the universe infinitely loved all these people, whether they knew Him or not. We prayed for the millions who by day hurried here and there in the beauty, prestige, and dazzle of that "City of Angels."

On that clear night though, everything twinkled in a calmer, quieter way for as far as the eye could see. The experience made me wonder about the reasons for Jesus' lament over the city of Jerusalem some two thousand years before. What did He see that they could not? "O Jerusalem, Jerusalem, the city that kills the prophets and stones God's messengers! How often I have wanted to gather your children together as a hen protects her chicks beneath her wings, but you wouldn't let me" (Matthew 23:37).

We came home from LA different than when we left. It was like that with every experience and encounter. Those years in Fort Worth were some of the richest of our lives. We grew exponentially in our faith as well as in our ability to see people more in light of God's love for them. Rich or poor, young or old, we were all made for the same purpose and with the same basic longings.

Over the years I had witnessed God's word as living and active, powerful enough to change hearts and reveal motivations. "For the word of God is alive and powerful. It is sharper than the sharpest two-edged sword, cutting between soul and spirit, between joint and marrow. It exposes our innermost thoughts and desires" (Hebrews 4:12). I had memorized that verse years earlier, but it never ceased to amaze me as I saw its process time and again.

In Fort Worth, I experienced God's truths in new ways as He showed me my heart, motives, and bents toward defensiveness, selfishness, fear, and pride. He reminded me that apart from Him I could do nothing. *Now, what part of "nothing" do you not understand?* I often heard Him say.

While at Hope, we learned to think about the brevity of life and that our days on earth are but a mist in comparison to God's eternal timeline. We learned the habit of evaluating choices in light of scripture and truly letting the gospel transform our lives. The psalmist reminds us to make the most of every day. "Teach us to realize the brevity of life, so that we may grow in wisdom" (Psalm 90:12).

Perhaps the concept that yielded our greatest growth was making ourselves accountable to people we respected in areas in which we wanted to grow. Accountability, we learned quickly, yields tangible, lasting results. Just ask any business owner, lawmaker, teacher, or parent.

And over those years, it became clear that serving others in Christ's name carried rewards we couldn't quantify. Jesus said the greatest among us is to learn to serve and that it is God who sees and rewards in secret. I think He turned everyone's concept of what it means to be great upside down by the way He lived and served the very people He had created. A friend of mine has often asked, "Have you ever noticed how God knocks Himself out every day just to show us how much He loves us?" Her simple question jarred something in me then and echoes its truth today. Tangible expressions of God's love are all around me, but my perspective is usually so narrow and focused on myself that I tragically miss their gift.

After several years of drinking it all in, we started to sense that our time at Hope was coming to a close. Knowing our heart for ministry, our pastor encouraged us to find a place to serve and to use the gifts and knowledge God had given us. He encouraged us to go and give our lives away. He was pushing us out of the nest.

Norm and I had learned all too well that you can't give away what you don't have and that you can't teach what you don't know. But we also knew God had given us so much and taught us timeless principles during our time in Fort Worth. The time had come to leave the classroom from which we had just begun to understand how to love others in Jesus' name. We questioned our own abilities and readiness. Had we learned enough to give away anything of value? Could God really use us in our brokenness?

We had been drinking from what sometimes felt like a fire hydrant of resources for a specific time and purpose. It had been a crash course in vision, servant leadership, and strategic living that changed us and would impact us more as the years went on. Even today we gratefully continue to draw wisdom and direction from our years at Hope as God shows new places to apply those principles while holding them loosely by His grace.

During our first rocky year of marriage, God showed us our neediness and total dependence on Him in every direction we looked. Over that first year or so, we had been given a pretty sobering glimpse of where we would have been left to our own devices. Out of a severe mercy, God painted us a picture of what it might look like to be in a marriage built on the false idea that we were mature enough, sweet enough, smart enough, exciting enough, strong enough, and good enough to meet each other's deepest needs. Trust me, it was not a pretty picture.

Part of Hope's vision is to be a sending base for those who want to plant churches and develop ministries for the furtherance of the gospel. Scores of ministries have begun all over the world as a result of their purposeful equipping of leaders. Though we felt inadequate and didn't want to leave the fire hydrant of life-on-life resources, we realized Harold was right. We needed to find a place to serve.

I am the vine; you are the branches. If you remain in me and I in you, you will bear much fruit; apart from me you can do nothing.
                                                              —*John 15:5*

chapter 18

Nashville: Our City of Firsts

Through a series of events and options, we chose to move to Nashville as bi-vocational church planters. We would be on a team with a couple whom we had known and grown to respect over our years at Hope, Fort Worth. Brad and Marty had moved there to pastor the church a few months earlier and were looking for people from Hope to join them. The Nashville church had studied the Hope network model for some time, was impressed by its effectiveness, and wanted to implement it in Nashville.

What a beautiful city! We loved the lush surroundings, the country and Antebellum atmosphere, and the way the music industry flavored everything and everyone. Like every city, Nashville had a personality and feel all its own.

We found a sweet apartment in Bellevue. Norm got a job at a local credit union in Brentwood. He was excited for the opportunity to learn a new set of skills. I heard that a large church in the area, Christ Presbyterian Church, was starting a school. It would launch the next school year and would be called Christ Presbyterian Academy. I applied and was hired to teach fifth grade. I was thrilled beyond description! Being one of their first teachers was an honor I will always cherish, especially when looking back at the academy's stature and influence decades later. Their school motto is *"Soli Deo gloria,"* Latin for "Glory to God alone." A perfect slogan.

What God did during the genesis of that school was nothing

short of miraculous. As new faculty and staff, we witnessed one specific answered prayer after another. For example, we prayed for paper and scissors; a few days later someone donated boxes filled with paper and scissors. Answered prayers became a common part of our morning updates. Like bold children who weren't afraid of a no; we just asked God for every little detail. The unity, excitement, and common respect among us was palpable. It seemed that God had handpicked each teacher and staff member for a specific purpose and to fit His plans for the school. That spirit of oneness set the stage for the years to come. Clearly, the God-given vision of CPA was bigger than all of us, and it was a joy to be part of its beginnings.

Our role with planting the church in Nashville, called Hope Community Church, allowed us to grow and stretch in new directions. Leading Bible studies; helping to establish home groups; and meeting, serving, and loving people creatively in our community filled our days. God used Norm's skills of leading worship and playing the guitar in our formal church gatherings as well as around many a campfire. I began spending time with some of the young women and helping them study the Bible.

We met and developed relationships with amazing people of all ages, ethnicities, and backgrounds. At one of our apartment complex's Friday night pool parties, we met Randy and Sallie Meinen, a couple about our age who had recently moved from Fort Worth. Discovering our Texas connection, we hit it off immediately. Becoming fast friends, we loved spending any time we could get with them. In the fall we invited them to come with us to a hoedown our church was having at the Thompson Farm. That evening other friendships were born, but Randy and Sallie seemed to develop a special bond with our pastor, Brad, and his wife, Marty.

Not long after that event, they began attending our church and studying the Bible together for the first time. They were hungry for truth and open to the gospel story. After several months, God reached their hearts and radically transformed the course of their lives. Over the next few years our friendship deepened. Their story is laced with one life-changing turn after the next. Their love for

Jesus naturally spilled over into their love for others and desire for them to know the joy and freedom in Christ they had found. Their quiet, steady faith was obvious and contagious. The impact Randy and Sallie have had over the decades on countless lives both in their careers and in their churches is incalculable.

Leading small groups in our home allowed us to grow close to young couples, singles, and families. Several of them became lifelong friends. That was certainly a place where God showed us how dependent we were on Him for every breath. Our faith grew by the month. A little icing on the cake was that we took full advantage of our love for sports and stayed active by playing more tennis and joining a city co-ed softball league.

Surrounded by country music legends, famous Christian artists, the Parthenon, beautiful parks, Summer Lights festivals, and the Opryland Hotel nearby to meander through for cheap date nights, Nashville was a magical place to begin our family. Amy Grant's "Tennessee Christmas" quickly became my all-time favorite Christmas song. Every time I hear it I somehow wind up kneading sourdough bread in my kitchen in Brentwood.

At twenty-nine, Norm and I decided it was time to start our family. There must have been something in the water at our church because Randy and Sallie, Norm and I, as well as Brad and Marty all found out we were having babies within weeks of each other. We all had so much fun comparing growing tummy sizes and morning sickness reports along the way. In our cases, misery, as well as joyful hearts, loved company. And we still have the pregnant profile pictures of our threesome to prove it.

So with all our Lamaze and CPR classes completed and Baptist Hospital's birthing center tour fresh on our minds, Norm and I felt prepared for anything. Mechanical and pure about every detail, we were soon to learn that we had a lot to learn.

With the due date right around the corner, I heard a repeated phrase, "No, just another false alarm," as Norm updated Brad and Randy after we had climbed back into bed following another mad dash. The false alarms came in handy though. We discovered the fastest routes at various times of day, and that there wasn't much traffic at all on the streets of Nashville at 3:00 a.m. My doctor had been right. First babies usually take longer.

But after several practice runs, the real day arrived. My labor began on my birthday. Everyone gushed with best wishes that I might have my first baby as a special birthday gift. Everyone, that is, except me.

Norm looked like a tourist on safari with that oversized camcorder on his shoulder. He followed me and filmed my every awkward move. "Let's get the side view one more time, honey," he said as he directed.

But me? I was in my own world, selfishly praying for mercy.

"Oh, Lord, please don't let me have this baby on my birthday. Never again will I have my own special day. I will always be the afterthought, sharing my time with the real star," I whined as my mind ran through scenes of me and my two friends sitting politely on the birthday sidelines, wearing fake smiles, and dutifully taking pictures of scores of little people wearing turtle costumes while devouring green cake with ice cream. Unaware of my tortured, self-preserving train of thought, Norm paced, encouraged, and filmed.

It seemed I would never get there. The intense start-and-stop labor seemed to have no end. After twenty-two hours and with the help of a merciful and wise nurse, who nonchalantly put his hand on my belly to help me push, our firstborn made his grand entry. Yes, the day after my birthday. "Thank You, Lord," I whispered for a thousand reasons. As the tears flowed, I reached to welcome our first, a son.

There were no words to describe what ensued between Norm and me in that moment. How could it be possible to love someone so completely whom you have never seen until now? After four years and countless experiences of seeing God grow and change us, our lives and marriage had just crossed over some unseen threshold. Together we entered a new realm where love and commitment are at the same time both divided and multiplied. We held in our arms what could only be described as the miracle of new life. In an instant we realized a heightened sense of excitement for our future. Now we were three. Joy, relief, wonder, and wordless praise flowed freely through those tears as we held our newborn. Outside on the streets of Nashville, the honking, noisy world stood momentarily still.

Nameless for almost a week, we finally crossed all the choices off our list but one. We gave him a name that means "beacon of light." Brandon has been that from his first breath. Born at eight pounds, ten ounces, he was our greatest delight.

We could hardly wait to introduce him to his room. Of course we had chosen a Carolina-blue rocking-horse-border for the upstairs nursery. Only days before, I had to be helped to my feet after painting the last brush strokes on the trim just before Norm finished cutting the hearts into the added railing on the changing table Norm had converted from an old dresser. Now the room was complete. Brandon was home.

Being a new mom who wanted to do everything right, I fed him every time he whined which was every two to three hours. That went on as the weeks became months. After about three months, I found myself exhausted and depressed from lack of sleep and the thousand emotions new mothers face. My life had quickly swirled out of control. Chaos ruled my days. This was not how I had it planned.

Thankfully, someone cared enough to offer wise counsel and mercifully, I had ears to hear. She explained that the pattern I had started would encourage an insecure, demanding child. While still in my nursing gown at noon, my wise friend brought me a book written by doctors which she had used with her children. "Here, sweet friend, read this," she said, noting my obvious fatigue and frustration. It may have been post-partum depression, but emotional swings and tears had become a normal part of my day. I wasn't doing well and word had gotten out. "I will take care of Brandon for you while you read this," she said.

My friend rocked and played with Brandon while I read and cried. I stared into a mirror of myself and my potential future as I devoured page after page. Her book explained from both a physical and emotional standpoint how and why to put babies on a predictable schedule as early as possible. Babies learn to trust if we can create for them some measure of routine in their days. The predictability created a comforting rhythm they learn from. The book laid out succinctly how it would look. I could put him on an every-four-hour feeding schedule since he was a healthy, growing boy.

After a little back-and-forth with my friend about some of my defensiveness and fears, and after a few more days spent reading and discussing the whole new idea with Norm, we made the decision to implement the schedule suggested in the book as closely as possible. We also saw her point that we had unknowingly established a schedule already. It was just an erratic, unpredictable one which Brandon himself had set. Without realizing it, we had put our child in charge. Babies aren't good parents.

My friend came over again to look us in the eye as she gave us our instructions. "This may be one of the hardest things you've ever done. Your emotions will try to pull you in and tie you in knots. He will get plenty of nourishment and adequate calories since he will eat at six, ten, two, and six. That's every four hours. Trust me, he won't starve. But you need to let him cry after you've given him his ten p.m. feeding. His little digestive system needs the rest too, just like yours and mine. But after three or four nights, he will sleep through the night," she explained firmly and with a confidence we could only envy.

"And Norm, you may have to put your foot down or maybe even tie Denise down when she tries to get up to feed him," she said in a tongue-in-cheek manner, looking over at me. "She will fight you tooth and nail because his screams will be blood curdling. He's a strong boy, and he is used to getting his way by now. You both need to resolve that you will not give in. This won't be easy, but it will bring back some sanity. Are you both up for that?" she asked, looking at both of us like Coach Roy Williams at halftime of the Final Four.

We soon discovered why we got Coach Williams that day. Brandon's screams were shrill, and they grew louder and more desperate as the first night wore on. The screams came in waves, tapering off into pitiful little whimpers. My mother's heart wanted to get up, go in and give him what he wanted. Everything in me sought to comfort my baby boy. I cried. I wailed. I sat up and prayed for him to sleep.

Norm, the strong, silent man that he is, put his foot down, literally blocking my way out of bed several times by swinging his arm over me. I wasn't sure I had what it took. He resolved to go the distance, but I was the weak link.

Then almost like magic, after two blustery nights of terror on the high seas and one somewhat better one, Brandon slept through the night. On the fourth night, we were not awakened until around six o'clock in the morning. He slept through the next night and then the next. And so did I. Imagine the immediate differences. My friend had been correct. Her little team had beaten the reigning champion of the night.

Implementing a schedule and heeding her wise counsel in that and other areas proved invaluable. Her confidence, strong coaching voice, and tough love through those uncharted waters were exactly what I needed. I know each family must choose their path and some may prefer the opposite, but peace was what I needed to regain my sanity and move in a better direction. Creating a workable schedule not only restored my sanity, but also our marriage.

"You cut your teeth on that first one," our wise coach told me. "You will sterilize every pacifier that hits the floor with this one, but by the third one, you'll just pick it up, rinse it off, and stick it back in before they can let you know it's out."

She was right. Truth is like that, proved over time. Her words held authority for us because I had taught one of her children and had seen the fruit of her wisdom up close and personal. She and her husband had led by example.

When I saw the immediate benefits of creating our new schedule, it became clear how that one concept crossed over into other areas of our family's life and health. Almost instantly I saw that the energies I had been giving to Brandon's insatiable demands to nurse had sapped me of the ability to invest in anything else including my marriage, friendships, gardening, and even the ability to sit and read a book. The chaos I had allowed to dominate our home was the antithesis of what I wanted our home to feel like. I had unintentionally allowed a ten-pound infant to become central and turn our once-peaceful home into a place we didn't recognize.

I later applied that same principle of creating order to other areas of discipline. Maybe that is why I never adopted the habit of counting to three to get our children to obey. We could just as easily train them to obey the first time we spoke rather than teaching them to wait until they heard the number three. Helping our children know they could trust the truth of our words was something we knew would translate into other arenas of their lives. We just tried to let our yes be yes and our no be no.

Most importantly, Norm and I knew that the trust they placed in us would one day be transferred to God. And as time went on, it was. Did we do everything we had hoped to do? Not even close. Were we always consistent? Not by a long shot. But we believed God would use even our meager efforts to point our children to Him for His glory. He would fill in the blanks and take up our slack. It was God's faithfulness we relied on, not ours.

After implementing our schedule and experiencing the results, I thought about a verse I had learned as a child. "For God is not a God of disorder but of peace." (1 Corinthians 14:33) Just about everything in creation mirrors order and rhythm if you think about it. Seasons, tides, plants, days, animal behavior, the laws of physics, and our yearly trip around the sun are a short list. Examine any part of creation. You will find wisdom in the order of all He made. I thought about how my soul felt frustrated and depressed in the bedlam and unpredictability. Maybe that is because the human heart longs for the ultimate peace of heaven and we will not rest until we find our rest in Him someday. Maybe we weren't designed to live in disarray.

Realistically, I knew it would be futile to think there would be no more times of chaos in our home. There would be plenty of messy, hectic days when the schedule was tossed out the window. But the peace and rhythm of following a plan made to fit our needs and goals would be the place to which we would now return; a little piece of heaven. That one major change rendered new life in our family I couldn't have put a price tag on.

It was in those early months with our firstborn that Norm and I acknowledged that Brandon (and any other children God might place in our quiver) was first and foremost His child. God had simply entrusted us to parent and train him up and to equip him with everything he would need for his real life and calling in Christ. We knew that knowing God and pointing our children toward their own relationship with Him were our real and main responsibilities.

We looked at our parenting as partnering with God. As parents, we were aware that our time of influence would be short and limited in scope. God would be their primary tutor. With our role in mind, we dedicated Brandon to the Lord when he was a baby. Like breathing, we raised Brandon to know and love Jesus and we read the Bible to him from before birth. When he was almost four, he made a personal decision of faith in Christ. He was later baptized.

Brandon was one of those kids you pray for a few more of. Having a wise and good heart, he was eager to learn and ready to please. He loved books and had limitless imagination and energy for play-acting. The first Bible verses he memorized were "Children obey your parents in the Lord for this is right" (Ephesians 6:1 NIV) and "But

the Lord said to Samuel, 'Don't judge by his appearance or height, for I have rejected him. The Lord doesn't see things the way you see them. People judge by outward appearance, but the Lord looks at the heart'" (1 Samuel 16:7).

Right off the bat, we realized that teaching by example was the only parenting model that would work. For years, I had observed that my students could spot hypocrisy from a mile away. I noticed how disrespectful and unmotivated they became under authority figures who said one thing and did another. It was doubly true of my own children. They don't miss a thing: facial expressions, rolling of the eyes, tone of voice, attitudes. Even our moods soak deep into a child's attentive heart. How many times has your child picked up on how you feel before you've said a word? Sarcasm, I noticed, was anathema to Brandon's spirit, so I prayed for the awareness to recognize it and use it sparingly if ever. Literal and honest, children serve as young accountability partners, making us better people and wiser parents. I think God weaves that rich element into families at no extra cost.

A major help with whatever we were doing as well as helping with his siblings when they came along, Brandon has always been a load lifter. Like most children, he had an insatiable desire to memorize and was ravenously curious. As a child, he memorized dozens of Bible passages, favorite poetry, and famous speeches. He had a penchant for acting out favorite stories, switching back and forth from his Peter Pan voice to his Captain Hook voice at will. The depth of his questions and his bottom-line answers kept us on our toes. The wisdom and remarkable thinking processes of children never cease to amaze me.

From before Brandon's birth, Norm and I had many late-night discussions about our children's education. When I was teaching in the public school system, several things concerned me greatly. I was struck by how much education had changed even over my lifetime. It concerned me that the basic core knowledge subjects had been dumbed down year after year. The watered-down rewrite of history in many textbooks alarmed me. We as teachers were being required to teach subjects that had more to do with social engineering than academics. Tenacious efforts to remove all mention of God from the public square and to make all truth relative had made their way into my classrooms. I saw it every day and it concerned me. Instead of equipping children to think for themselves using logic and critical reasoning, it seemed students were being told what to think and how to feel.

What had once been the clear distinction between right and wrong had undeniably become blurred, if not totally erased. It was clear, but no one wanted to admit it, much less address it. The non-admission became costly. Because of some unwritten rule, within just a few years, nothing whatsoever could be said by a teacher about good and evil. I was required to teach classes on situational ethics which further blurred the lines for the precious children who sat in my classrooms and asked questions I was not allowed to answer honestly. I witnessed respect for authority in general eroding more each year.

A Christian apologist, Ravi Zacharias, once said, "These days it's not just that the line between right and wrong has been made unclear, Christians are being asked by our culture today to erase the lines and move the fences, and if that were not bad enough, we are being asked to join in the celebration cry by those who have thrown off the restraints religion had imposed upon them. It is not just that they ask, we accept, but they now demand of us to celebrate it too."

For those and other reasons, Norm and I made the decision to educate our children from home. We wanted to be the ones to hear them read for the first time. It was our choice to make the investment in their classical education to see the light bulbs come on in the middle of a chemistry experiment, a math problem, or their history lesson. As parents, we wanted the privilege of watching the reverent silence as they stood before the Grand Canyon, the Alamo, or the Lincoln Memorial. And most importantly, we wanted to equip them to know God, the highest call and deepest need of mankind. Looking back, I realize the entire homeschooling experience was a gift from God to our whole family, most especially to me.

After high school, Brandon chose a college that offered a unique major in philosophy and worldviews. He went to London for an apologetics course at Oxford that focused on the works and teachings of Søren Kierkegaard and C. S. Lewis. After graduation from college, he moved for several months to Honduras as a mission pastor.

Currently, he teaches math in the Middle East, where he met a brilliant young woman from Germany. They married a couple of years ago and just had our first grandbaby, Zoey. I am a total mess just thinking about holding my first grandchild when they come home in a few weeks.

Really? A grandbaby? How could that have happened this soon? Didn't he just learn to sleep through the night? I have said that our children come in the front door, do a few laps through the house, and walk out the back door before we even turn around. I can tell you firsthand that this is true.

Whatever is good and perfect is a gift coming down to us from God our Father, who created all the lights in the heavens. He never changes or casts a shifting shadow.

—James 1:17

chapter 19

Carolyn, Mentor and Friend

A mentor is someone who knows more than you in a skill or field of some sort and is willing to come alongside to help you learn. In Christian circles, this practice is often called "discipleship." I have been fortunate to have had several mentors, who gave of their time and expertise to walk with me for various lengths of time. It was during our time in Fort Worth that Norm and I began to grasp the value and many long-term benefits of someone older and wiser willing to come alongside and help us grow.

Carolyn Teague was one of those for me. She still lives in Fort Worth and is a legend in many circles of student ministry and campus work in the United Stated and around the world. She is one of those rare people who make you feel like you are the only person in the world when you are with them. To me it was like knowing Billy Graham.

I met Carolyn when we first moved to Fort Worth. We had been going to Hope Community Church for a while, and I kept hearing people talk about her love for Jesus and about how gifted and wise she was. Her shadow of investment in people stretched long and wide. She had been on the original team of people who had started the church in a home.

I had learned that she was an author, a teacher, and a prayer warrior who had memorized much of the Bible. Carolyn had given her whole life to helping people, especially students, come to know

Jesus better. Everywhere she went, she left a lasting wake of godly impact. She had been working with college students as either a professor or a student ministry director for years. I had grown to respect her and admittedly was intimidated by her before we met. My intimidation wasn't just because of her reputation but also because friends had told me she asked really penetrating questions. Perhaps I thought I might meet her and she would ask me a penetrating question; then I would just stand there like a deer in the headlights, looking silly.

But when I finally got to meet her, it wasn't like that at all. She was warm, genuinely gracious in an everyday sort of way, fun loving with a contagious laugh, and curious about me. Carolyn had a magnetic yet humble personality. People just wanted to be with her. I became one of those.

When we moved to Nashville, she was one of the people I would miss the most, not because we were best friends—we weren't—but because being around her made me a better person. Carolyn made me want to reach a little higher, give a little more, listen to people more attentively, be more curious, and ask better questions. Her good and gracious heart had become contagious, even at a distance.

It wasn't much more than a year after we moved to Nashville that I learned she had accepted a job offer to work at the Home Mission Board located in downtown Nashville. She would be relocating short term and would attend our church. Everyone who knew her anticipated her arrival.

Within a few weeks of her arrival, Carolyn and I arranged to have lunch, and I asked whether she would consider mentoring me in the areas of scripture memory and better application of scriptural principles to my marriage. After praying about my request and checking her already packed schedule, she agreed to meet with me on a weekly basis. We decided I would drive downtown and meet her right after work hours in her office building for about an hour each week. Many times we had something simple to eat and just sat on the carpeted floor while we talked, laughed, and dug deeper into the Bible.

We both set some goals. Since one of mine was to memorize certain scripture passages, she coached even my worst attempts at getting them verbatim. And of course, she usually had some penetrating question each time we met that made me think outside my boxes.

"What do you think Jesus meant when He told the disciples He had food they didn't know about?" she might ask as we read that passage.

"How did Jesus treat the woman caught in adultery? What do you think He wrote in the sand that made all her accusers go away one by one when they had stood there only moments before, rocks in hand, ready to stone her?"

Then, holding me accountable to my goals, she asked how certain principles we had been studying might apply to areas of my marriage in which I had expressed a need to change.

It's funny when I think about it; there wasn't a single time when I felt silly.

Over those next few years, Carolyn and I became close friends, encouraging and challenging each other in various areas of desired growth. Once after Norm and I had moved back to North Carolina, she surprised me with an invitation to accompany her to a Christian women's conference in Oklahoma City, for which she had made all the arrangements. That was just one example of her ongoing ministry in my life.

Recently, I got one of those voice mails where someone is obviously trying to disguise his or her voice by talking in a phony British, Mexican, or Bohemian accent. I immediately knew it was Carolyn. Usually she called using her signature British voice. This time she used a higher-pitched, nasally, very southern voice. "Yes, ummm, this is the National Search Committee, and I'm just looking for someone who can go on a cross-country trip with me. All you have to do is hold the door shut for about seventeen hours and not fall out. Okay, well, sorry I didn't get you. I'll catch up with you later. Bye, now."

She had been referring to the time when she moved back to Fort

Worth after her work in Nashville was complete. She had asked Norm and me to travel with her to help with her move. The day was set. Her lease was up. Norm and I packed the last of her stuff into her car and the U-Haul. Our next-day plan was for me to ride in the car with Carolyn while Norm led the way in the truck.

But the weekend forecast was for freezing rain and sleet. All of us hoped it would miss Nashville. It didn't. The fast-moving cold front ran from Texas through the state of Tennessee. On moving day, with set deadlines to meet, we awoke to a gray day of frigid temperatures, a sheet of ice, and freezing rain. They made for a miserable day to travel.

As we prepared to leave, we realized her car doors had frozen shut. The only one we could pry open was the driver's side door. So being the good friend I was and knowing we were indeed Texas bound with no Plan B, I climbed across the front seat and slid to my perch on the passenger side.

While we battled the treacherous road conditions, our main dilemma happened about an hour after we got on the road. Somehow my passenger side door swung open. But because of the freezing rain and frigid temperatures, it wouldn't close again no matter what we tried. It just slammed as if on a solid block of ice. Even with Norm's most industrious efforts to remedy the situation, the door simply wouldn't close. It would be an understatement to say I looked panicky.

"Maybe you could just hold it closed like this," Carolyn instructed while demonstrating her fancy door-closing moves as though I didn't know my only option. I was well aware by then that if I valued my life, I would need to put all those farm girl muscles to good use. There was nothing I could do but step up to the plate and take my best swing. It was me against the elements, and at that moment, the elements had the edge.

So, bundled up dutifully and gripping a door handle for seventeen unending hours, I sat with heater blaring. We experienced mile after mile of monotonous road with Carolyn cracking highway mishap stories and facial-mangling jokes as I viewed wet pavement just inches away through hopelessly fogged windows. It was one long, hilariously infamous trip the three of us will never forget. We still write marginal notes or leave phone messages, offering to travel cross-country in similar fashion "for old times' sake." As of yet, there have been no takers.

Now that entire vivid memory was back in a flash as I smiled while listening to her unmistakable voice on my recent voice mail. Good friends are like that, though. You can just pick up where you left off or somewhere along your familiar way, rehearsing a memory or an ongoing joke shared only by the two of you. Friendships like that are a priceless gift, never an intrusion. I think it's because there aren't many friends like that.

The heartfelt counsel of a friend is as sweet as perfume and incense.
—Proverbs 27:9

chapter 20

New Opportunities

Norm was offered a teaching position at Christ Presbyterian Academy the year Brandon was born. He seemed more than glad to leave the banking industry admitting it wasn't where his heart was. Teaching middle-school math and Bible and being with young people eager to learn seemed a much better fit. I watched as Norm thrived and found a sense of purpose and joy in working with his students. His fun-loving ways and youthful enthusiasm quickly endeared him to both students and faculty. Norm was an enthusiastic teacher, a skilled musician, and a natural athlete. He jumped in with both feet. CPA was one of those unique schools that felt like a family of dedicated individuals all on the same team.

Because of that closeness, it was a difficult choice when I decided to retire from teaching in order to fulfill my other childhood dream: to be a mother. Being a teacher at heart, I decided I could manage both dreams for a while. I structured my day so I could tutor CPA students in reading and math while still being there for my newborn. Tutoring allowed me to keep my toes in the teaching waters and bring in some much-needed income.

The year after Brandon was born our church went through several difficult transitions. Growing pangs maybe, but everyone felt the upheaval. The biggest change occurred when our friends, Brad and Marty, unexpectedly decided to leave the church to begin a new ministry in another state. It had been a gut-wrenching and difficult choice.

Loving them as we did, the news hit us hard and prompted us to question our purpose for being there. Our stride was broken and Norm especially struggled to find it again. We prayed for perspective. The love we felt from our small group and the way the church supported us through that time was invaluable. But even with their encouragement, Norm continued to question our reason for being in Nashville. It seemed a door had closed he no power to reopen. So as he wrestled, he prayed for clarity and direction.

We had been in Nashville almost four years when we discovered baby number two was on the way. We were elated and ready. New dreams and expectations filled our days. Brandon immediately began making plans and gathering toys to welcome his new baby brother or sister.

Norm realized that God doesn't waste anything. He began to understand that the stirrings and unrelenting questions were for a purpose. After prayer and seeking counsel from trusted friends, Norm chose to pursue the possibility of entering student ministry. All his gifts, training, and past experiences could be put to use and working with college students would be a strategic way to impact the world for Christ. Just one question loomed. How would he get his training and experience?

Within a few weeks of seeking the answer to that question, Norm was offered a one-year internship opportunity to work alongside a friend who was an experienced campus ministry pastor at Texas Christian University in Fort Worth. The internship would prepare him for full-time campus ministry and give him the experience he needed. After many late-night discussions and a little wrestling with each other, we decided to take another leap of faith. Norm accepted the internship for the next school year. His responsibilities would include conducting Bible studies on campus, designing student activities and helping students grow in their faith. I was happy that Norm was following his heart, while in the same breath choosing to move right then felt insane. But we were young and free; and at least one of us loved the thrill of the unknown.

I was relieved that we weren't going to move right away. We would need to put the house on the market and pack everything up. Spring was right around the corner. The baby was due the first week of June and would be two months old by the time we were scheduled to move in August. We figured that would give us plenty of margin.

Maybe it was because I was pregnant. It may have been selling the house, or leaving everything I had grown to love about Nashville. I think it was all that and more, but this time I couldn't get excited. I didn't know what or how to pray. Leaving our city of so many firsts with more questions than answers, was one of those times the emotions just would not come.

And the Holy Spirit helps us in our weakness. For example, we don't know what God wants us to pray for. But the Holy Spirit prays for us with groanings that cannot be expressed in words.
—Romans 8:26

chapter 21

It's Not Supposed to be This Way

Everyone has hurdles, walls, mountains. We all face challenges we think might undo us. And there are times in all our lives that are private—times either too painful or too joyful to put into words. Such was the next era for us. For over seven years, indescribable joy alternated with pain so sacred and inexpressible that it almost seems a betrayal to write of them here. The Bible tells us that in this life, we see only part of what is going on. We get only hints and tastes of what God is up to most of the time. Like seeing the trailer of a movie or reading the Cliff Notes of a classic, we get only snippets here on earth. But someday we will know the greater story. Someday we will see the panoramic view from a new, unclouded perspective.

I open this curtain only a bit. Like me, you will grasp only a partial view. But maybe someday we will both get a bottomless popcorn and drink as we get the full-length version with credits, backstory, and all those far-reaching ripple effects about which we had no idea. Here is the story.

The last few days of May, leading up to the first days of June, always bring it back. The joyful anticipation. The sudden jolt. The hollow depths of numbness and disbelief. The searing pain mixed with raw unleashed anger. The innumerable questions without answers. The slow-moving images. The shattered dreams. The unexplainable peace. Mine was a mother's private journey.

Our second son died from a cord accident just before birth. Friends sat in the waiting room praying through the night as I delivered our stillborn baby. The doctor diagnosed a cord kink possibly from a sudden onset of gestational diabetes.

He was perfect. A beautiful baby boy, he weighed eight pounds, ten and a half ounces, and measured twenty inches long. He was the spitting image of his big brother. There was no denying he was ours.

My questions flowed like my tears. "Oh, Father, why? Why us? What did we do wrong? Are you punishing us for some unconfessed sin?"

I clearly remember arguing and screaming out to God in my anger. "Lord, with so many discarded and aborted babies, why take one that was so wanted? We loved him even before he was born."

"Wouldn't we have taught him to know and love you? Oh, Lord, I don't understand!" The cries and guttural questions came like sniper bullets from every direction. They continued unabated. No doctors, nurses, friends, faith, or family could offer any relief. Our questions rang hollow with no answers. Only silence. The hours passed. As desperately as I searched, no comfort came.

They put a large blue teardrop on the outside of our birthing room door. I remember thinking that no one had words. There was nothing to say. Our faces and hearts refused any gesture of comfort. The one thing we wanted we couldn't have.

The staff came and went, caring for us the best they knew how. Without warning a neonatal nurse entered our dimly lit room and said, "Norm and Denise, please know we mourn with you. All of us are sorry for your loss. We have prepared your baby for you. You can keep him in your room if you would like to hold him for a while and say goodbye. The choice is yours."

Either decision felt wrong. We agreed we wanted the opportunity to have our son with us as long as possible. As I sat upright with tears flowing and uneaten food on the hospital tray, I held our second son, stroked his hair, and spoke aloud thoughts that had been held behind a dam of emotion. What came next were hollow-sounding words wishing for an audience.

Norm crawled onto the bed beside us. We both wept as we held each other and voiced for the last time the dreams we had spoken for the past nine months over this beautiful likeness of ourselves. Ours were every parent's multicolored dreams. The child we had rejoiced about only hours before would soon be veiled and given back to people we didn't know and would never see again.

In that brief window, we had held death in our arms. Perspective found little entry into our room. Grief controlled our every word. When the time came, we had the nurses snip a piece of his hair and take a picture for us to keep. Handing him back felt like handing off part of my soul.

Over the next few hours, I began to sense a mysterious parallel that superseded my grief, confusion, and anger. It was like an overlay. Without removing the pain, a strong presence carried us through those days that we felt like limp rag dolls. The murky waters that threatened to carry us downstream didn't overwhelm us. Though our hearts lay shattered, there was an awareness deeper than our pain. Greater than our sorrow, it buoyed us above despair. Even with unanswered questions pounding at our door, I was aware that I did not grieve as one who had no hope. God's presence kept us from going under and being swept away. He breathed for us and stayed the demons of terror, anger, and doubt that taunted at the door.

Hope Church members and all our students, fellow teachers and staff at Christ Presbyterian Academy loved us in countless ways. They called and sent letters expressing love, encouragement, and concern. People we had known from Texas, the Carolinas, and elsewhere sent cards and gifts and made phone calls. They had rejoiced with us at Brandon's birth. Now they wept with us as we wept.

In our grief we had sought and received advice from a friend who owned a local mortuary. I remember his words well. "People don't know what to say when infants die. It is customary and best for you to request that only family and close friends be present with you under the tent and for the burial. That way you spare so many people the undue pain of trying to comfort you," he explained.

"Whatever you think is best," we told him. He was the professional, and I had no energy to argue his reasoning and experience. Swimming through each hour, we were just too numb to make those kinds of decisions. So it was announced that those were our wishes. We would have a small, private funeral. For days almost every decision was made for us. Norm and I moved in slow motion from one moment to the next.

One of the few things I recall about the day of the funeral besides my father-in-law asking why I had those dark circles under my eyes, was sitting in our mauve, overstuffed den chair with Brandon on my lap. He had just turned two. Mature and wise beyond his years, even then he amazed us with his insights. Sensing my heaviness, he seldom left my side. He mostly just snuggled close and rocked with me in silence. But that morning before we left, he took my face in both his little hands and said, "Don't cry, Mommy. Justin is in heaven with Jesus. You know we will see him again someday." And with that he retook his tattered "bankie" in his mouth and resumed his place under my chin.

On the day of the funeral, we made our way to Woodlawn Cemetery in Nashville. I remember walking toward the funeral tent on the arm of my wordless husband. He carried Brandon in his opposite arm. He is a strong man, and it was never clearer than during those days when he grieved differently yet in a manner no less broken.

The tiny casket as my focal point, I didn't notice those gathering along the cement drive that snaked through the cemetery and circled around us.

The pastor spoke a few words of comfort and led in a song or two. He then read the two letters I had written. The first was to friends and family, the other to Justin. But when we all stood at the end of the short service to sing the song we had requested, Norm motioned toward a scene still etched in my mother's heart.

All around us like a great cloud of witnesses were scores of cars with friends standing respectfully beside them. As if they had known my wishes, they had come anyway. They were there to love us. But out of respect, they granted our request for privacy. When we began singing, "Jesus loves me this I know, for the Bible tells me so," people emerged from their cars and sang with us. Many had their hands over their hearts as they grieved with and for us. I was moved beyond tears by the outpouring of love we were given on that most difficult day of our lives. My only regret was that I had no ability to show my gratitude or voice my thanks at the time. Having friends there meant more than we could express. I learned a valuable lesson I will never forget. We are not made to be alone. It is especially true in times of grief and loss.

Here are the letters I wrote. A pastor/friend read them at the funeral. The theology may not be perfect, but they expressed my heart at the time. I was thirty-two.

Letter to Family and Friends:

> Justin Burke Williams. Born June 1, 1989. (8 lbs. 10 oz., 20 inches long, dark brown hair)

> Dearest Family and Friends,

> Over the past four days we have experienced the deepest, most thorough pain we have ever known. We have also experienced first-hand that unexplainable peace that really has passed all our ability to understand. God has given us His peace as He said He would in John 14:27, "Peace I leave with you; my peace I give you. I do not give to you as the world gives. Do not let your hearts be troubled and do not be afraid."

> God's great love and faithfulness have been demonstrated to us; and much of that He has chosen to do through you. He has spoken clearly and audibly through every prayer, phone call, visit, casserole, flower, and mile crossed to be with us at this time. Every gesture of sympathy and love has carried us

from one moment to the next. We can never express how deeply you have ministered to us. So we simply say, "Thank you!"

We also want to publicly thank God for making available to us His rich love, and for the personal relationship we have with Him. We have voiced to Him our questions, our anger, our overwhelming pain, our doubts, and our fears. He has listened and has enveloped us with His Presence. His Presence is providing light to get us through the now.

Our prayer for all of you is that you, too experience the reality of a relationship with the Living God, and that you know the joy and peace that we know even in this time of inexpressible grief. God too experienced the loss of a son, His only begotten Son so that you and we could be called the children of God. He grieves with us now.

We love you,
Norman and Denise

Letter to Justin

Dearest Justin Burke,

We wanted to write these things to you to publicly acknowledge your life and just say aloud what we have only said in private. First of all, we gave you your name as a heritage to your life. Justin, which means "just and upright," we gave to you because we believe God is good and just. He does all things well. "The lord will perfect that which concerns me; your love, oh Lord, endures forever. Do not abandon the works of your hands," is what Psalm 138:8 says.

Then, Burke means "one who dwells in the fortress." We know that you now live in the fortress of God's abiding presence. "In his presence is fullness of joy, at his right hand there are pleasures forever more." Ps.16:11.

Your mother, daddy, and big brother are thankful that you will never have to experience pain, or guilt of sin, or sadness. And we are grateful that you will always dwell in the fortress.

You were only with us for 39 weeks, yet you silently brought joy and sparkle to our home. We are so thankful for every week. We do not believe that God was the one who took your life from us; because he is the one who gave you life and without him we wouldn't have had the joy of those weeks at all. But, he has allowed you to come early to your fortress. And we now grieve not being able to do all the things with you that we had hoped for and dreamed of.

There will never be a day that you we won't think of you and long to just spend time with you. You are very special to us. No one can ever take your place in our family. We look forward to spending thousands and then millions of years with you in heaven.

As we say every night to your brother, Brandon, "Justin, Daddy loves you, and Mommy loves you, and Jesus loves you." We always sing this song to Brandon and we would like to sing it for you now.

[We had those in attendance sing this song with us.]

"Jesus loves me this I know, for the Bible tells me so. Little ones to him belong, they are weak, but he is strong…"

We love you,
Mommy and Daddy

————————————

That simple song expressed all that needed to be said as we walked to our car surrounded by the love of that cloud of witnesses.

I have often described grief as a series of circles spiraling outward from a tightly wound intense center. As you move from the middle over time, the intensity gets less, but the emotion is cyclical and never gets erased.

I remember I almost felt guilty when the laughter returned, like I was being disloyal to Justin for being able to find anything worth laughing about after that.

A few weeks after the funeral, our church had a retreat at Fall Creek Falls, one of the many beautiful Tennessee state parks. The guest speaker was Henry Blackaby. He and his wife had just been through an excruciating trial themselves. Their only daughter had been diagnosed with terminal cancer and had undergone treatments. Their story and prescient teaching in the book *Experiencing God* were timely and began a healing and deepening process for both of us.

Somehow on Saturday, we wound up sitting at a table for four with the Blackabys. Over lunch, they asked some questions that revealed they knew a little about Justin's death. I think I was at the point where I could begin articulating some of what had been bottled up for weeks.

I quietly poured out my heart about Justin's death and spoke a few of my many questions aloud for the first time. Because I knew there weren't any answers, I had not really expected any. It almost seemed a betrayal to my faith to give voice to raw thoughts and agonizing questions. Like a dam breaking, I shared some of the anger, the doubts, the pain, the feelings of betrayal, the confusion, and the abandonment. The main question that day was, "If God really loves us and is sovereign, how could He allow a cord accident to happen to an innocent baby?" But I really think I was asking, *How could this happen to us?* I think in my pride and anger I was really saying, *Why us? After all we've done for God? Hadn't we earned better treatment?*

They listened and cried with us. Then Dr. Blackaby said, "Norm and Denise, I don't know why this has happened to you. You are asking some of the questions we asked. I won't pretend to have the answers to all your questions. But it really helped me when our daughter was going through her cancer treatments to picture her illness and pain with the backdrop of the cross of Christ as the focal point. Holding everything up to the light of what Jesus did there allows Him to give us perspective when we don't have answers. But God did answer all the big questions at the cross. Someday when we meet Him in heaven, He may give us the answers to all the questions we still have. Or it may not even matter then."

Though they didn't erase the pain, his words were like salve for my broken heart and wounded spirit. It was a beginning place to receive a viewpoint I had never considered before.

Another phrase I took away from that weekend that really helped was, "Why *not* us?" Dr. Blackaby dedicated an entire session to that question. Now that one changed our perspective and gave us a lot to chew on. We still chew on it from time to time.

It was hard to see anything through the fog of grief that threatened to consume me back then. We were emotionally still raw, and though our feeble steps forward seemed miniscule or sometimes two steps back, God had reminded us that weekend of His eternal love for us. Undeniably clear, His love and overcoming power had been demonstrated at the cross and in His resurrection three days later.

Justin's death was the starting point where God began to unravel our piecemeal theology of trading our good works for favor and blessings. Like John Bunyan's Pilgrim when he began his journey with his fingers in his ears, I had to block out the voices calling me back. The journey toward having freedom and knowing God would require daily reminders of the truth. God's ultimate goal for His children is to form us into the image of Christ. All of us are in process. And that process will not be completed until we get to heaven, where we will clearly see without those Coke-bottle glasses, through which we peer now.

Now we see things imperfectly, like puzzling reflections in a mirror, but then we will see everything with perfect clarity. All that I know now is partial and incomplete, but then I will know everything completely, just as God now knows me completely.
—*1 Corinthians 13:12*

chapter 22

Learning to Trust in the Dark

Almost two months after Justin's death, we packed our now bigger U-Haul with a little help from our friends. Friends are load lifters in more ways than we can know, aren't they? Norm had accepted an internship as campus ministry staff at TCU. Chuck and Kathy and Miss Jenny, some special load lifters from our church, had decorated a piece of tag board with "Fort Worth or Bust" and attached it to the front grill of our U-Haul. There were streamers on the fenders and gifts covering the front seat as we pulled out of our driveway and waved sad goodbyes to them and to our city of so many firsts, our home for over almost five years. I remember feeling little excitement but great waves of fear and sadness.

Perhaps the scariest part was that we hadn't yet sold our house. The lumps in our throats were real as we thought about having our tight budget and paying monthly on two houses. So we left with a prayer on our lips despite our realtor's grim warning not to get our hopes up. "Just keep in mind this is a flooded buyer's market," she said.

All the way there, I kept wondering about what my new home was going to look and feel like. I had seen it on video, but the images had faded. Norm had flown out a few weeks earlier to search for a house and get all the details of his new campus ministry position figured out. After viewing a few video clips, we chose a house only two blocks from the TCU campus. It was a tidy brick Tudor in one of those older neighborhoods where kids ride bikes on the sidewalks and people take walks at all hours of the day. Norm said it had plenty of room for student gatherings and Bible studies. The kitchen was cool. And it had a fenced-in backyard with a swing. Hmmm?

Norm agreed to stop and call our friend Sallie to let her know the minute we arrived in Fort Worth. She was our contact person and liaison for all the people back in Nashville, and she served as keeper of the keys for our new house. I will never forget Norm's response. He came running across the parking lot of that old, greasy service station, grabbed me out of the car, and swung me around, yelling, "Sallie got a call from our realtor. Our house sold somewhere between when we left Nashville and here. We got our asking price. Yahoooo!"

Time seemed to stand still as we laughed, cried, and twirled, thanking God and dodging potholes in the parking lot before coming back to reality and our little caravan, with Brandon looking on starry eyed and half asleep in the back seat.

Selling the house was of course an enormous load off Norm's back. That clearly answered prayer, and others like it came in handy more than once in the next few months. They served as tangible bookmarks of God's attentiveness to our needs and pleas for help. The timing also spoke volumes to me.

Before three months had passed from that parking lot celebration, I found myself lying on our bedroom floor facedown in a sea of royal-blue carpet. My palms were up and out in front of me as I cried out to God. I lay there, half weeping, half listening for any hint of comfort. Emotionally weary and physically worn out, I knew I lay at a crossroads that would determine how I lived the rest of my life. I remember sensing the presence of God there with me. The words Jesus spoke to His disciples in John's Gospel seemed His question to me that day. "Are you also going to leave?"

I remember thinking about that question for a good long while. My mind considered all my options. I don't know how long I was there. But later I cried out, almost squirming on the floor, "Where else will I go? You have the words of life. Lord, though You slay me, yet will I trust You" between sobs so deep and high pitched I didn't recognize my own voice.

Why was I so discouraged that I found myself facedown on the floor? Because in late August we discovered we were pregnant again. "It's just too soon. I'm not ready," I protested, holding the pregnancy test in disbelief.

Still weary from the grief of our loss, we gathered our wits and began preparing for another baby. Then, in late October, at about twelve weeks along in that pregnancy, while having lunch with a friend in downtown Fort Worth, the cramping and bleeding began.

"You are most likely miscarrying this baby," the doctor said matter-of-factly as I turned to leave his office. "Just go home and wait until it's over." I wondered whether delivering the news of miscarriages had become so commonplace to him that he had lost his once-deep compassion, or whether he had always been so cold and emotionless.

It was a prolonged process that went on for days. In the end I lay in a hospital bed after the D&C, trying to quote scripture to my friend, Janet, as she sat and cried with me. The gift of friendship is a priceless treasure. Her quiet presence with me that day meant more than I had the ability to convey.

Physically and emotionally devastated, I found myself without words again. Over those next few weeks, my spiral-bound journal served as confidant and therapist. Writing provided a medium for the unrelenting questions, anger, confusion, and compounded grief. Here is one of the entries:

Dec. 1, 1989

> Weary from the pain of losing our second son just before his due date and our recent miscarriage, I still falter over boulders of debris and wreckage that I thought were neatly piled up along the side of the road in my journey called the "grief process." Yet just this morning, a full six months after Justin's death, I

found myself in the shower with a quickening urge to call my doctor and cry, "What if I had had one more ultrasound? Would that have saved my baby's life?"

I thought I had exhausted all those "if only" questions six months ago. But somehow even now, I am ambushed by thoughts that hide in the most unexpected places: behind shower curtains, under my pillow after my husband says goodnight, in grocery store aisles while walking by the baby food jars, or in the joy held in every other mother's arms while walking through the mall.

Life does go on, of course. For me the process has been somewhat like a spiral. Each rung of the spiral getting a little further away from the intensity of the inner circle. The pain becomes less severe over time, yet it's just as real. Often the process of grief just repeats itself but in lesser degrees.

The answers are few and the questions many. My faith in a sovereign God has deepened over these months. We live in a fallen, imperfect world; and as long as we are here, we suffer many effects of that state of imperfection. God's grace and joy, it seems, have been shoveled into a heart destitute and empty of anything but pain and confusion.

Someday, I hope to be able to shout with Paul, "Oh death, where is your victory? Oh death, where is your sting?" But for now, I am content in singing "The Wheels on the Bus" with my two-and-a-half-year-old."

It was around that time that someone gave me a copy of C. S. Lewis's books *A Grief Observed* and *The Problem of Pain*. I devoured them both and began searching through the Bible with renewed hunger. Through those books and in my insatiable search through the scriptures for answers, God began showing me that much of what I believed about Him was a house of cards. Though overall I had built my life on the foundation of Jesus's finished work on the cross and His power over sin and death, there were places in my heart that revealed I had either added to the truth of the gospel or was not at all living in the light it provided.

Reading those books was the first time I recognized that my belief system contained fissures that had to be addressed if I desired to experience God's truth and live in the freedom He had promised. For the first time, I saw that my theology consisted of part sound Bible teaching; part opinions from pastors, respected evangelists, magazine articles, or novels; part cultural influence; and part my own feelings and notions of what a loving God should act like. Without realizing it, I was working hard to please God in order to win His favor.

Waiting for the next shoe to drop, I had ignored the truth that Christ had dealt with all my sin at the cross. I had forgotten that Jesus had taken all my shame and guilt on Him when He suffered as the sacrificial Lamb of God. I was living as though He had not conquered death by rising from the dead. Too much of the time, I lived as though freedom in Christ were only an illusion.

One other debilitating theological problem was that I thought I had been a pretty good girl so far. I wasn't that bad. On the comparison chart, I was certainly somewhere in the middle. I had been deceived into believing in my own goodness. Considering all I had done for God, surely I deserved much better treatment than this. Most of my life had been given to serving others. Since a child I had memorized God's word and hidden it in my heart. I knew all the rules. There were few anywhere who followed them better than I did.

I had never considered that I had been trading with God as though I had something to offer. Lies and half-truths too numerous and complex to count were eating my lunch and stealing my joy. It would take someone greater than I to shine the light of truth on them and help me undo their ripple effects. It would require the grace and mercy of a loving God.

At that moment, though, not only was I confused about what I thought I knew about the promises of God, but my dreams were in the process of being shattered. And worse, I had no idea how to put them back together and move on.

That's where I was that day when I found myself on my face, weeping and weary before God. Like Humpty Dumpty, my hopes for my future had fallen off the wall and had shattered into too many pieces to count. All around me lay the remnants of a theology that was no longer working. I held up one piece after another with question after question. *What about the rules? What about being obedient to the things You told us to do? What about Your command for us to choose life? What about Your rewards for following You? Don't You see me? Don't You care?*

That day on the floor, my attempts to find answers had been met with a strong, loud, glaring silence. It was the kind of silence that caused me to fall on my face in worship and called for total surrender with my hand over my mouth. The tablet that held what I thought I knew about God and my ideas of how life was supposed to work out lay broken at my feet.

Unlike Humpty Dumpty, though, God Himself would help me with the pieces. He would show me a better way. He isn't the kind of Father who gives us what we are screaming for just to get us to be quiet and stop our whining. He is the good Father who knows the future and equips us for what we cannot see. His way of rebuilding my knowledge of Him had a lot more to do with making me into His image for His glory and my true happiness, and it had much less to do with following impossible lists of rules.

In His mercy, God showed me there were no magic formulas and that walking by faith was deeper and more mysterious than checking boxes or trading good deeds for perceived blessings. By His grace and daily reminders, He would free me from my transactional theology. He would draw me deeper into a real relationship, where

I could count it all as loss for the high calling of knowing Him and the power of His rising.

I had twice walked through the valley of the shadow of death. Those experiences had shown me that though death threatened to rip from me all hope, joy, and peace, it was only a shadow pointing to the Giver of life and to my longing for a time when pain and death will be no more. I was learning to trust through not only the miscarriage and Justin's death but also the death of a vision. All my life I had longed for family. Norm and I had dreamed of and planned for a house full of children. Here I lay, feeling that vision slipping out of my reach. I had no control over anything really. Letting that sink in was one of the moments in my life in which I was aware of what Jesus must have meant when He spoke of giving up my life in order to find true life in Him.

That day on the floor was one of those points of no return. Through His strength I made the choice to trust God with whatever my future held. By faith, I had given up trying to figure it out. Though I wasn't healed from the pain, my hand and my heart were open to Him, who was the Way, the Truth, and the Life.

As I got to my feet, I remembered what I had heard Elisabeth Elliot say once at a conference I attended. "Just do the next thing." So day after day during those dark years of learning to trust in the dark, I just did the next thing. I made the decision to trust God's heart, even though I couldn't understand His hand.

This is the old Saxon poem, from which Elisabeth Elliot learned that phrase:

Do it immediately;
Do it with prayer;
Do it reliantly,
Casting all care;
Do it with reverence,
Tracing His Hand,
Who placed it before thee with
Earnest command.

Stayed on Omnipotence,
Safe 'neath His wing,
Leave all resultings,
DO THE NEXT THING.

Then Jesus turned to the Twelve and asked, "Are you also going to leave?"
Simon Peter replied, "Lord, to whom would we go? You have the words
that give eternal life. We believe, and we know you are the
Holy One of God."

—John 6:67–69

chapter 23

We're Moving Where?

For a girl who didn't love moving, I was getting plenty of opportunities to learn how. The bottom line is that I don't like change. I especially don't like leaving friends and the familiar. Truthfully, I long for home. Maybe you are like that. In addition to my longing for home, my introvert tendencies pull me into my own space probably a little too often. Most days, if given the choice, I would rather stay on a familiar front porch and read a good book. Over those first twenty years of our marriage, the porches changed size, shape, and views sixteen times.

On the other hand, Norm thrives on change and adventure. He never liked letting the grass grow too long before he was ready for the next challenge, which I came to realize in those days usually meant we were moving.

After only a year as campus ministry intern, Norm was ready and equipped to lead. He put out résumés all across the country to see what might open up for us.

Before we knew it, there were several offers from universities seeking a campus ministry director with his skill set and heart for students. We put things in high gear as we visited various campuses around the country that spring and summer.

"I wish God would just make those clouds form the shape of a *C* or a *P* just to make it clear about where He wants us to move. I know He could give us a sign, but I'm beginning to understand that the longer we walk with God, the fewer signs and wonders we get. Mystery seems to take the place of clarity. I think it has something to do with growing us up. He wants mature kids," I said to Norm one evening as we walked hand in hand down a country road in Lock Haven, Pennsylvania. We had flown there to interview for one of four campus ministry opportunities. Each option brought with it a long list of pros and cons, which we pored over on each return flight.

Colorado had been my first choice. There were many dreamy reasons. In fact, in my heart and mind, the U-Haul was already unloaded, and I was picturing our little family on the slopes of Aspen.

Dinner dishes had been put away, and Brandon was getting his pajamas on when Norm returned from his day of prayer and fasting over the decision before us. When he rounded the corner into our kitchen, his words rang with a resolve I have seldom heard from my gentle man of few words. "Honey, we are moving to Missoula. I think it's our best option all the way around." That night I whipped out the atlas and looked it up. Yep, Missoula was definitely in the continental United States.

And so it was decided. Here was another time God would have to change the desires of my heart. There were no letters in the clouds, but Montana would be our next home. Our job description was simple. We were to rekindle a student ministry on the University of Montana campus. Working through the Baptist Student Union, we would partner with a local church to create an atmosphere in which students who wanted a relationship with God or growth in their faith could do so through our Bible studies, mentoring, and various planned activities and group events.

Deep down I sensed this move would be the most challenging yet. We would soon be entering a whole new world and planting our lives in what would feel like a foreign country for this southern–born–and–bred girl who had already felt the stretch of enduring big city traffic, experiencing culture changes, leaving Tennessee Christmases, and living far from family.

Something in me knew adjusting to life in Nashville, Houston, and Fort Worth would feel like falling off a log compared to the major shifts in thinking and culture that awaited us in Missoula.

It was a beautiful town surrounded most of the year by snowcapped beauty. The convergence of five mountain ranges created a bowl, which kept the clouds nestled within, often making the winters long and dreary. We learned that some who lived there suffered from a light deprivation disorder resulting in depression.

But we came to realize that in the short weeks between when the spring snows melt out of the yards and flowers shoot up, until the fall snows begin again, there is a bright, not-too-hot, sunny brilliance to Big Sky Country that makes the long winters bearable, if not a little enjoyable. For Montanans, the bitter cold is one of the things that accounts for their toughness, fortitude, and resilience.

Besides getting accustomed to the frigid temperatures, sunlight deprivation, and long snow season, there would be major mental adjustments. Some were remembering little details like thinking to wear bear bells, checking the hillsides and trees for mountain lions and bobcats while hiking, and reading the headlines about the latest mountain lion or grizzly sightings. We would develop a taste for elk, bear, and moose fresh from someone's most recent hunting trip.

A wonderful friend, who became like a second mother to Brandon, killed a bear soon after we moved there. A great cook, she was more than excited to offer us some of what she had prepared for supper. She and her husband were both avid hunters and members of the church we attended. Thankfully, they took us under their wing and tutored us in the ways of Montanans. The Wenderoths and others like them were those who spared us much embarrassment, showed us special out-of-the-way places, and breathed life and outdoor adventures into our three years there.

The Lord says, "I will guide you along the best pathway
for your life. I will advise you and watch over you."
—*Psalm 32:8*

chapter 24

Mother's Intuition

Soon after arriving in Missoula, I discovered I was pregnant again. At around three months into the pregnancy, the amount of movement I felt and my rapid growth concerned me. I hinted more than once to my doctor that I thought there was action enough for two in there. I had actually prayed that we might have twins after the loss of two babies and the growing awareness that I wasn't getting any younger.

"Yes, most women have the same concern at this stage. You are only measuring a centimeter or so bigger than average, Denise. I really don't think there is any way you could have two in there," said my doctor when I was about sixteen weeks along. With that, I attempted to brush off my suspicions as wishful thinking.

But at twenty weeks my concerns persisted. I called the doctor again to say, "I know you have been clear. You assured me there is almost no chance there is more than one baby. I know I may be suffering from pregnancy paranoia, but there is much more movement this time. And I've been extra nauseous throughout this entire pregnancy. Would you just humor me and let me rule out my gut feeling that I have two babies in here?"

"Okay, if you feel that strongly, let's go ahead and put you on a monitor tomorrow morning," said Dr. Furniss, matching her words with my emotion.

During the exam the next morning, she hooked me up to a monitor so we could listen to the baby's heartbeat. Our eyes widened as the swishing sounds grew clear. Initially, we heard one heartbeat. But every now and then we could hear what sounded like either an echo or two heartbeats. "That may just be an echo, but let's send you over for an ultrasound just to make sure," she said, looking over her charts.

Norm dropped me off at the medical complex that afternoon and darted off to run a few errands, knowing it would be a while before the procedure would be finished. In the darkened ultrasound room, I lay quietly as anxiety mounted awaiting the technician. My mother's intuition would soon be proven one way or the other.

When he entered the room, I wondered whether the young technician was old enough to know what he was doing. But my fears were quickly forgotten as he skillfully took control, squirted the gel, and began instructing me as he slowly pressed and moved the wand from side to side over my belly. I was relieved and began to relax. At the same time, he turned the monitor so I could watch the screen with him.

It wasn't long before I heard, "Yep, there's a lot going on in here. There's one head, and … there … is the other. There's an arm and another and another, and that … makes four. And here are two legs and right there, see? There are the other two." Having no prior knowledge of my thoughts, he spoke as though I already knew the news and he was simply confirming it. The tears began flowing as I silently watched the moving images of two precious babies on the screen.

Within minutes, Norm was ushered into the darkened room, and the tech reviewed the whole process I had just seen. Norm has always been a man of few words, but he took silence to a whole new level as those pictures told the story. The reality of life with three children, all under the age of four hit him like a ton of bricks.

Soon realizing the unfolding situation, the young man offered, "I will leave you guys here for a bit while I let your doctor know these results." With that he left the lights as they were and closed the door quietly behind him.

My tears increased as I recounted what we had just witnessed.

Norm, obviously in shock, leaned harder against the wall and sank onto the heating unit under the room's only window.

"All I could see when he was talking was double dollar signs. Two of everything. Cribs, diapers, food, strollers, college tuitions," he said in what was almost a mumble. The color had drained from his face as his mind ran the possibilities.

We said little as we walked from that building back to our doctor's office. Everything felt overwhelming. Dr. Furniss had received the report and said she would see us right away. As we walked in, she offered her congratulations and quickly the mood lightened as we joked at my gut feeling being proved right.

On the phone with my mother later that afternoon, I asked, "Mother, what has two heads, four arms, and four legs?" I sat, waiting for either puzzled silence, or for her request for another clue in my little game of twenty questions.

"You are going to have twins," she said, not needing the other nineteen. You could have blown me over with a feather. "You know there are six sets of twins on your grandmother's side of the family," she went on without waiting for me to confirm. She spoke calmly as if someone had already given her the news.

Could my mother have had the same gut feeling? We were always close that way; thinking each other's thoughts. Sometimes I called home, only to find out we were cooking the same meal for supper, or had both planted our gardens that day. The thoughts raced as I pondered her composure with such news.

"No. Mother, no one ever mentioned that part of our family history. That's unbelievable!" I said as my mind began churning out more questions for her.

When the dust settled, Mother seemed happy for us. At the same time, I could tell she held our announcement with caution as we finished our mother-daughter discussion. With every conversation to share our news, our friends and family were guardedly excited. Truthfully, so was I.

*Let all that I am wait quietly before God, for my
hope is in him. He alone is my rock and my salvation,
my fortress where I will not be shaken.*

—*Psalm 62:5-6*

chapter 25

Heaven Meets Earth

What is it about faith that Jesus so often pointed it out and commended it? His stories and parables were constantly highlighting it for all to see. Why do you think faith was the requirement for us to know Him and experience eternal life?

Perhaps it was seen best in His gentle reprimand when His disciples wanted Him to send the children away. Jesus instead drew a child, perhaps an infant, from the crowd. I can imagine He may have looked directly into the little one's eyes when He told the disciples they had to become like this if they wanted to enter the kingdom of heaven. Here is the verse to which I refer:

> Jesus called a little child to him and put the child among them. Then he said, "I tell you the truth, unless you turn from your sins and become like little children, you will never get into the Kingdom of Heaven. So anyone who becomes as humble as this little child is the greatest in the Kingdom of Heaven."

— Matthew 18:1–4

That scene has become a faith lesson for the ages. Jesus's example to the disciples must have stopped them in their tracks. It required a turn in their thinking. I call it one of their many pivotal moments.

His teachings were revolutionary then and continue to turn our modern paradigms of greatness and what is really important upside down.

We can all cite pivotal experiences, moments that come out of nowhere and make our world stand still without warning, shifting our entire perspective from that moment on. When Brandon was three and I was pregnant with the twins, we had one of those experiences.

Norm was downstairs in his office, working on upcoming student events. It was the day after Halloween. The usual jack-o'-lantern full of candy served as the centerpiece on the kitchen table; it awaited our rummage sessions as we decided what we had a hankering for next. Brandon sat with crayons and coloring books as we discussed his latest imaginings, and I made a stab at answering his newest series of questions.

I was in my usual multitasking mom mode. Having just cleaned the kitchen and started a load of laundry, I was making a peanut butter and jelly sandwich at the kitchen counter when I noticed Brandon walking silently, almost trudging into the kitchen with an unusual look of helplessness mixed with fear on his face. After asking him a quick question, I realized he couldn't speak and was trying without success to breathe. It was obvious he was in a state of silent panic.

I yelled for Norm to come quickly. He bolted up the stairs and assessed the situation. We became an instant team as we performed the CPR steps we could remember for choking victims.

When he in his panic refused to open his mouth, we tried prying his jaw open, but that proved worse than useless. We performed the Heimlich maneuver for children as we had practiced on those plastic dolls in our classes. Nothing changed. Repeating that process, we called his name, trying to keep him conscious and with us. Still nothing. We attempted different positions. Norm applied more force. Still no change.

"Brandon, buddy, stay with us!"

Then, in desperation, Norm turned our son upside down and over his knees while I tried to dislodge whatever was caught in there. By that time, Brandon was turning blue, his body limp, his eyes glazed. We could tell he wasn't conscious of our efforts. We both also knew after a short discussion that an ambulance would take too long to get to us since we were on the outskirts of town.

Having flashbacks of holding our lifeless child just over a year earlier, I simply cried out in a loud voice, "Lord Jesus, help us!"

The next thing I knew, I said emphatically, "I know I'm not supposed to do this, but I am going down his throat with my finger. It's the only choice left!" We put him onto his back and pried his mouth open. Norm stepped back as I got on my hands and knees and did the CPR mouth sweep with my finger, looking closely for any signs of what might be the problem. Then, even in our dimly lit kitchen, I could see at the back of his throat a shiny, round object, which I immediately knew was one of the chocolate balls from the jack-o'-lantern. Securely lodged, it was blocking his airway. I used my index finger and tried to hook it forward, not really caring at that point whether I scratched his throat. We knew our child was dying, and this was my last effort to change the inevitable.

When my finger hit the chocolate ball, it was too slick and slimy and too embedded to hook, but my efforts dislodged it and sent it on down. Panic then hit me like a lightning bolt. Almost immediately, though, Brandon's body convulsed forward. He gasped for air as he began to choke and then to vomit, scream, and cry. These were all unbelievably welcome, frighteningly beautiful signs of life.

The next few minutes were filled with few words but many grateful sobs of joy and disbelief as we held and comforted our precious son in the middle of our kitchen floor. Brandon's color, which had been blue from the waist up only moments earlier, soon returned to normal as he began to breathe deeply and recover in Norm's lap.

I next called his pediatrician, who told me to bring him in for an exam to see whether the chocolate ball had gone into one of his lungs. After his thorough exam and X-ray and hearing what had just happened, the doctor told me I had certainly saved my child's life. Thankfully, his lungs were clear. A very sore throat was his only repercussion.

Still shaking and weak from the whole episode, we gratefully returned home with our precious three-year-old gift of life. As we returned to peanut butter and jelly on the counter, dirty dishes in the sink, and laundry in midstream, our view of all things had changed, our perspective had been forever altered.

I recollect the vivid details of that event not just to gain renewed gratitude for the vibrant life of my son but to remember the larger lessons for my life today. The lessons I took from that day when the veil was rolled back for a moment and I could see heaven meet earth from my kitchen floor are many. They include gratitude and respect for life with its mystery and uncertainty; a sincere appreciation for God's faithfulness to all His promises; a better perspective on what is important; a deeper sense of His presence in every moment of my day; a keener awareness that I am surrounded and filled by a good, powerful, ever-present help in time of trouble; and more confidence to come boldly to ask, seek, knock, worship, and be.

Maybe that's why I don't like the phrase "God showed up." I know what people mean, but it seems to suggest He was somewhere else and then just magically showed up in the nick of time. It hints that God is like a genie in a bottle whom we can control or expect at our door when things get tough. God told us He would *never* leave us or forsake us. He either meant it, or He didn't.

When I appealed to Jesus that day in my impotent humanness, I don't believe He was summoned. He was already there with us. He didn't just swoop in from some faraway assignment all out of breath. Also, I believe it was the grace of God that gave me the prompting, even to cry out. In that sudden, unforeseen life-or-death moment, I cried out loudly for mercy and help, never doubting He heard my desperate voice. Looking back, I believe it was also He who in His mercy supplied the strength, courage, and lightning-quick wisdom we needed in that crisis.

Because of Adam's sin and the brokenness sin has wrought, we live in a world that is not as it was intended, nor as it will someday be again. Along with nature and all the ages, our souls groan and cry out for God to make sense of the ravages and ramifications of sin's tentacles abundant all around us. Someday it will not be so.

Although many stories don't have our desired outcome, history is replete with those where heaven touches earth and we experience God's intervening hand. No doubt you have some of your own. I am forever grateful to include this one in that ever-growing list.

Be strong and courageous! Do not be afraid and do not panic before them. For the Lord your God will personally go ahead of you. He will neither fail you nor abandon you.
—Deuteronomy 31:6

No one will be able to stand against you as long as you live. For I will be with you as I was with Moses. I will not fail you or abandon you.
—Joshua 1:5

Teach these new disciples to obey all the commands I have given you. And be sure of this: I am with you always, even to the end of the age.
— Matthew 28:20

chapter 26

A Thanksgiving and
Christmas to Remember

The first three months in Missoula flew by as Norm and I began building relationships with our core group of three or four students. As their numbers grew, the energy in our room multiplied. Students brought their unending questions and beautiful curiosity, along with their opinions, funny quirks, and boundless energy. They captured our hearts.

The sweet rhythm of having a constant flow of young people over for meals, game nights, and sometimes no particular reason had begun. According to my journal, we had about nineteen people around our table at Thanksgiving for traditional turkey and dressing with all the southern trimmings. Some of the girls came over, wanting to help with every little thing. We did it all, including the main dishes, gravy, sweet potato soufflé, and pumpkin pies. The guys put all their muscle and charm into making the cleanup a breeze. They all served as prime entertainment for Brandon as he shadowed their every move and soaked in every never-boring minute.

On the day after Thanksgiving, I began having what I initially thought was from too much turkey and dressing combined with the over-the-top hilarity of student antics. When the pains persisted and became more intense, I knew the problem was more than that. What began early afternoon as simple Braxton Hix contractions with mild tightening sensations continued for several hours. When their intensity became more regular and closer together, our concerns heightened.

"This can't be happening. I'm not even twenty-six weeks," I said to Norm, who was working in the den. Soon I was timing what I concluded had become full-fledged contractions.

"Our babies aren't viable yet. But these are not simple contractions," I said as we decided what to do.

"We need to call the doctor," Norm said.

I already had the number in my head.

"I'll meet you at the hospital. Get there as soon as you can," said Dr. Furniss after I explained to her how my day had progressed.

When we got there, the contractions squeezed stronger and became painful. I could tell my body was going into labor. Everything from there swirled around me as they put me in a bed and began the examination process.

Dr. Furniss checked my cervix and discovered I was already dilated to three centimeters. Her eyes told me all I needed to know as she said, "I think you may be losing these babies. I am going to order an ultrasound and put you on a magnesium drip to see if that will stop your contractions. Denise, we're going to invert you and put you head down, feet up. Hopefully that will get the weight off your cervix. Let's see if we can get these contractions stopped and get you through the night. I'm going to do everything possible to save these babies. How does that sound?" she said, walking quickly with me. She ordered the ultrasound as they wheeled me into a room and began the IV drip. Ours was an experienced, take-charge doctor. That was one of her many skills, for which Norm and I both grew more grateful by the second.

The ultrasound revealed that Baby Girl was head down and already engaged in the canal. Baby Boy was pushing her down and causing her to press on the cervix, thus the early contractions. It seemed he wanted out now, and she was blocking his way.

"I guess this means I'm not going back home tonight, honey," I said to Norm as he stood helplessly by my side. He then left to make arrangements for Brandon to stay the night with friends.

The next few days were some of the most intense ones of my life. People all over the world committed to pray for us and the twins. We felt the prayers since there wasn't much either of us could do but pray and wait and pray some more.

The contractions continued to escalate despite the increases in the medications that were meant to delay preterm labor. Dr. Furniss, who was usually smiling and lighthearted, seemed half pastor, half drill sergeant when she entered my room a few days after my labor began.

"Okay, we have made it through a critical couple of days. From here on, every day you can give me counts. These babies need to stay put as long as possible. What I am going to say will not be easy to hear. But it's just what we have to do. You're going to have to lie here and remain as motionless as possible, Denise. I don't want you to put even one foot on the floor. I don't want you to flex your toes. You just need to keep your babies cozy and warm in there for as many days as you can. You're unique in that you are extremely sensitive to stimuli of any kind. Every move you make seems to trigger more contractions, and contractions are what we want to stop altogether if we can," she said, ending with a look that was both sympathetic and laser focused. There was no doubt she meant business.

My commitment to do whatever it took to give the twins a fighting chance matched hers. I would become a willing incubator. My doctor and I, with equal resolve, became a team to win this uphill battle for the life of two precious babies.

The drug I was switched to because of a reaction, terbutaline had many side effects: shortness of breath, heart palpitations, and rapid eye movements. Because my eyes fluttered, my vision blurred so much that I was unable to read. That condition frustrated me because devouring as many books as possible had been the one thing I looked forward to while bedridden and immobile.

Each afternoon when my doctor made her rounds, she came into my room. After examining the long paper roll, which had recorded the contractions that day, she asked, almost like a district attorney,

"Hmmm, what were you doing between ten and noon? And also at three this afternoon?"

"Norm and Brandon were here this morning. Brandon played and then took his nap beside me. Then someone from the church stopped by around three o'clock for a short visit. Why?" I said, thinking I had done something wrong. The monitor had reflected more intensity in the contractions at those times. Many, she pointed out, were overlapping each other. That was unacceptable.

The next day, a "No Visitors" sign was put outside my door, and all visitation stopped except a thirty-minute daily visit from Norm and Brandon. Brandon was no longer permitted on the bed. Eventually there was no television. The doctor ordered the lights dimmed because it seemed even light increased the contractions. Who knew someone could be so sensitive to every little thing?

I couldn't read. I couldn't pass the time with my favorite shows like *The Andy Griffith Show* or *Jeopardy*. Now this? Loneliness and boredom set in. I put Paul's admonition to pray without ceasing into full use. Unanswered questions flowed like rain. There were days when I felt completely overwhelmed with the heaviness surrounding the possibilities of what lay ahead. The most difficult part of my days became what was forbidden: no showers, no visitors, no sunlight, no sounds except the beeps and monotony of machinery. I guess I have always had the tendency to want what I couldn't have, and now freedom to do as I pleased topped the list. But the kindness and encouragement of nurses and staff as they came and went became daily treasures to my eyes and ears.

As days rolled into weeks, other moms and newborns came and went. You can imagine that I got to know the staff pretty well. Pretty soon they started to get my dry wit and sense of humor. After a while, some of the nurses challenged me to declare names for my babies. They were tired of calling them "Baby Boy" and "Baby Girl."

In the early nineties, a sitcom called *Newhart* still ran in our area. One particular episode had become iconic in our family. So after much thought, I announced, "Okay, I've decided. Our son will be named Darrell, and our daughter will be Daryl. The only difference will be the spelling. That way Brandon can say, 'Hey, I'm Brandon. This is my brother, Darrell, and my sister, Daryl.'" Everyone knew the line and thought my idea was hilarious. Many mornings after that, the nurses and staff entered my room, asking about little Daryl and Darrell as they lovingly patted my tummy. We had all become like family. Of course, it was a running joke that gave a little levity to an otherwise heavy time. Our babies' real names would be decided in due time.

December came, and with it winter storms. My room had a window that looked out onto another building. But in between was a small courtyard that allowed me to watch the snow level rise. One day I noticed activity in the courtyard. My curiosity soon turned to tears as my three-year-old and his amazing daddy packed and rolled mounds of snow, creating and dressing the cutest pregnant snow woman and her child ever built outside a hospital window. They made sure the pregnant profile was obvious from my vantage point. The fine silhouette of our snow woman warmed the hearts of all the nursing staff and became a new conversation piece on those cold days.

Then the week before Christmas, Norm and Brandon marched in tandem into the room, donning lumberjack attire, proud smiles, and a perfect Christmas tree just for me.

Norm told me the story of their slippery van ride through the woods in search of the perfect Christmas tree. They had spotted the one they wanted. He and Brandon took turns elaborating about how when Norm, saw in hand, poised ready to top the huge spruce, Brandon cried out from thirty feet below, "Daddy, I gotta go."

Brandon was zipped up tightly in his new snowsuit that made him look like the Michelin Man. The little fellow couldn't get that darned zipper down with his mitten-secured hands. Norm, as the good daddy, abandoned his almost-secured alpine trophy, shuttled down the tree, and rescued his son, who was squirming desperately in knee-deep snow, just in the knick of time. Norm then rescaled the evergreen, felled his prize, and made his now-familiar way down. In the silent natural grandeur that is a Montana forest, the two proudly hauled their prize to our minivan. And there it stood, ready for tinsel and lights. Did I mention Norm's cape and halo?

That story made the rounds at the hospital, embellished with a few grizzly and mountain lion additions for days as people came in and out of my room, keeping track of the various-sized packages accumulating around our now-handsomely decorated, glowing tree. There was one oversized mysterious package that stood tall in the corner. That one had us all guessing since no one seemed sure of where it had come from or when it had been delivered.

Mom and Dad Williams flew out to be with us at Christmas. They were such a gift to us all as they loved on Brandon and made life much easier for Norm. Understandably they had hopes that they might be part of the big day. But Norm and I prayed we could get closer to the due date, still months away.

During those unending days, I remember one particular time I was praying, or most likely complaining, about the loneliness and all the twists and turns of recent months. I believe God gave me a mental picture of what He had been doing and would continue to do. Through the tears of my depression, which on some days rolled into my room like a thick London fog, I saw a big potbellied stove. Slowly the little door on the front of the stove opened, and God shoveled something in. It wasn't an actual vision, but because I think in pictures, it came at a time when I most needed tangible encouragement.

At first I thought He was shoveling in coal, but then I realized the substance was my daily portion of grace mingled with courage and patience. The story of when God sent the Israelites their daily portion of manna in the desert came to mind. Clearly, I was given what was needed for that particular day. There was just enough. It was He who decided the measure and when I needed more.

From that point on, I often imagined the stove door swinging open at crucial moments. Like when I felt I could lie perfectly still no longer or endure one more day of muscle pain. Or on the days when boredom overwhelmed me, God would shovel in more strength, patience, and grace to stay my course. Amazingly, that picture of the stove kept me there and prevented me from losing my mind. Jesus spoke sanity into my insanity and assured me He was with me through it all.

Whether it was the multiple sticks it often took to find one of my rolling, hiding veins, the depression I felt from the lack of seeing the sunshine and blue sky, my pleas for the nurses to sneak me down to the baths for a mercy shower, or the loneliness I felt from being in solitary confinement day after lonely day, God spoke to my heart with that still small voice, assuring me that He would never leave me or forsake me and that He was my joy and strength.

Sometimes He spoke through cards and letters or the prayers of friends and family. Other days encouragement came through the words and acts of kindness of caregivers, and the many people who helped with meals for Brandon over those months. Whatever form it took, that still small voice reminded me like He did with Hagar, that He saw me and cared about me, even in an obscure hospital bed in what often felt like a foreign country, where I knew almost no one, and no one really knew me.

Reminding me of promises and truths I had believed since childhood, God breathed assurance and hope into my worried hopelessness. Though not audible, His voice was sometimes the only one I heard. Like daily bread, I discovered it was the only one my soul required. For perhaps the first time, I learned that real intimacy with God is often learned when circumstances feel dark.

During those long days, God also revealed to me that He only gives me grace to handle what is on my own plate. He never gives me the grace to handle someone else's burden. And likewise, He doesn't give others the grace to handle mine. I think that's why we are told never to compare ourselves to others. A sovereign, able hand tailor-makes what we need to fit each circumstance.

On Christmas Day we had a big family celebration of opening gifts around my bed. Norm's parents were there along with our legendary tree, a few nurses, and our doctor's family. To my utter amazement, she and her husband had been the mystery Santa who had delivered that enormous package which had kept us all guessing.

Turned out it was a super fancy twin stroller. Norm and Brandon ripped into it, discovering it was equipped with sunroofs and mag wheels to boot. A real beauty. What special friends she and her family became over the years!

Brandon tore into his gifts with proud parents and grandparents looking on. We were hoping and praying that next year there would be three healthy kids rummaging through presents and playing around a normal-sized Christmas tree with its own story, minus the mountain lion and grizzly sightings.

But the gift that outshined them all was the beautifully wrapped box some of the nurses on the floor delivered that morning. They grinned from ear to ear as they strolled in like the three wise men bearing gifts for the baby Jesus. "We got you a little something. You guys are special to us, and we love your whole family. Maybe these will help you remember us after the twins are born and you get to go home," they said beaming ear to ear.

"Oh, you guys are too much," I said as I began opening their package. Inside were two tiny infant T-shirts. I held them up for all to see. The pink one had "Daryl" in white bubble letters on the front, and blazed across the baby blue one was "Darrell." We all laughed uproariously then and for days afterwards!

What a thoughtful gift for twins, in whom they had all invested greatly. Those little shirts were one more encouragement for me to keep lying there not moving a muscle for as long as possible. We had all become team players pulling together toward the same goal post. I felt their cheers that Christmas day as I had in a thousand caring ways every day of my now-month-long stay.

When you go through deep waters,
I will be with you.
When you go through rivers of difficulty,
you will not drown.
When you walk through the fire of oppression,
you will not be burned up;
the flames will not consume you.
For I am the Lord, your God,
the Holy One of Israel, your Savior.

—Isaiah 43:2–3

chapter 27

A Blizzard in a Blizzard

New Year's Day came and went without fanfare. My contractions had grown more intense in the days after we welcomed 1991. Each time Dr. Furniss left my room, she would add, "Just one more day," as she patted my legs and held my eye for courage. That had been her hopeful mantra to me for six weeks now. Lie still. Keep those babies in there. That was my only mission.

January, as usual, brought heaps of snow and frigid temperatures to the northwest. Norm's parents were disappointed they didn't get to meet their grandbabies, but they left just in time to escape a full-fledged blizzard, which hit the morning after they left. Experiencing a Montana winter was something I had yet to do, which was one bright spot of being where I was since I hated cold weather. Blizzard conditions had kept the hospital quieter than usual. Even Norm and Brandon were unable to leave the house for a couple of days.

But on January 9, the doctor read my monitor data and decided to check my cervix. Her quick check and widening eyes gave her fears away. "Today's the day, Denise. You're dilated past the point of waiting any longer. Let's get you ready." She called in the nurses, and everything swung into high gear.

Ready or not, the time had come. I had done all I could. With lots of teamwork, the babies had stayed put past thirty-two weeks, which were beyond anything my doctor had anticipated that night back in November. She was hopeful that all the shots I had been given to speed their growth and mature their lungs had done their magic. Now all we could do was hope and pray for a few more miracles. We called Norm, who was hunkered down at home in the storm.

After a close call with my reaction to a drug, I was prepped for a C-section, and everything blurred from there. Within an hour several doctors and nurses worked meticulously, murmuring quietly on the other side of a cloth barrier they had created for me. Norm held my hand and tried to assure me everything was going to be all right. I'm pretty sure beneath that stone wall of courage, his fears and feelings of helplessness matched my own.

Then, just minutes before midnight, a male voice announced, "These are big babies! Didn't you say we were at thirty-two weeks?" I could hear Dr. Furniss's voice concur and calmly direct the others in the next steps. As they soon took the first baby from the room, my emotions burst like a dam that could no longer keep its flood contained.

Two minutes later they removed baby number two. The hushed silence as they left the room spoke volumes as Norm and I listened for any hint of encouragement. None came. Their quick actions and serious tones betrayed any optimism. They were obviously working against the clock as it stood sentry on the cinderblock wall. I lay cold and scared as doctors switched their attention to me.

Later in the hallway during my recovery from surgery, a doctor I didn't know came over, put his hand on my shoulder, and said in a matter-of-fact tone, "Your little girl is a fighter. We think she will probably be okay. But your little boy won't make it through the night. His lungs are just too weak. I'm sorry." With that he caught my eyes for a brief moment, then turned and walked down the hall. I never saw him again.

Alone with that news and unable to move, I prayed God would give me strength to make it through whatever lay ahead. I had already held death in my arms and began anticipating that picture repeating itself. As I felt the tears streaming down my face there on the gurney, I remember opening my hand as if to say, "I'm still trusting here in the dark." And at the same time I was asking, "Are You there? I'm so weary. When will all this stop?"

My heart was breaking at the prospect of losing another baby. Flashbacks of a funeral tent and lines of people comforting us went through my mind, and my body trembled in fear. Icy fingers of dread and terror gripped deep in my throat. I could hardly breathe. I felt air leave the room as my emotions began spinning out of control. Then right in the midst of that spiral into a deep abyss that threatened to swallow me into its darkness, a peace I cannot describe swept over my trembling mother's heart. It superseded everything else.

It was as though someone had come in and told the lions to go back into their dens, and they had tucked tail and obeyed. An opposing army had come to my rescue. A quiet calm replaced the fear. The churning waters became a sea of glass. My mind stopped inventing scenarios. The tremors ceased. I came out of the death spiral, and the immobilizing terror abated. My breathing became more normal.

What came next were unexpected feelings of peace and confidence. Not confidence in myself or in some mystical force. I grew keenly aware of God's abiding presence right there with His weary, fearful child lying on a cot in a cold, dimly lit hallway during one of her darkest nights. It was a switch I can't explain except for the fact that God is who He said He is. And He really does hear our cries for help, even when our voices are gone. I experienced God as a very present help in my time of trouble.

The blizzard outside the hospital was a picture of what had been going on inside my soul. Would I trust as emotions swirled and icy doubts and accusations of God not caring or hearing me howled nonstop in my mind? Would He be enough for me in the dank chill of yet another circumstance over which I had absolutely no control? Would I walk away? Would I keep my hand open in the face of another death, or would I make a fist and shake it back at God? Not that He couldn't have handled the fist or would have loved me less had I chosen it, but mentally and emotionally I stood at a crossroads. It was another pivotal moment.

My awareness of His presence was like what happens when you turn on a light switch in the black of night. The darkness had to go. It wasn't that I was assured Jordan would live. I had no idea what the future held. It was deeper than that. It wasn't at all about circumstances or religious ritual. Nor was this about whether everything would turn out the way I thought best. It wasn't really about me at all.

I was learning that there was more to my life than dictating to God how it should be and being happy only if it worked out that way. There was no attitude of, "Lord, what have You done for me lately?" or "What did I do to deserve this?" But rather it was about what He had become to me in the silence and in the dark. A relationship had long been forged over my lifetime, but through these years of pain, God had made Himself real to me in ways that now translated into peace and a solid place to stand. I was not alone.

When I embraced the peace and comfort of the Lord that night, it felt a little like letting go and taking a giant leap off a cliff into a place I had never been. I found the place I had fallen into was a place where I had wanted to be but had never known how to find.

I discovered light accompanying me in the darkness, hope where little or none was offered, and freedom to surrender to a good God when everything swirling around me wanted to call Him cruel or sadistic. Mercifully, my hands were being wrenched free from gripping the ruinous theology of trading good deeds and right thoughts for God's favor. He was trading my burden for His, and His was light in comparison.

I was learning what it felt like to look beyond circumstances, feelings, and opinion into the heart of God. I was entering a new place, and it was different from what I had thought true happiness might feel like. There was another level of life I was detecting, an infinite expanse that begged exploration. It felt like what James had been talking about when he encouraged us to consider our trials joy. It had nothing to do with the direction of my smile. Somehow I sensed it was only a foretaste, a glimpse of a pleasure so bountiful it would take an eternity for my stubborn, finite mind and aching heart to grasp.

I remembered Henry Blackaby's words to us that day at Fall Creek Falls, when I sat weeping over lunch. He had encouraged us to look at everything with the backdrop of the cross. He had talked about the fatal blow Christ had dealt to death and to our separation from God. Through my tears, holding all my fears and pain against that scene of Jesus's loving sacrifice outside Jerusalem ushered in perspective, peace, and hope as the blizzard swirled all around me on that long January night.

Dear brothers and sisters, when troubles of any kind come your way, consider it an opportunity for great joy. For you know that when your faith is tested, your endurance has a chance to grow. So let it grow, for when your endurance is fully developed, you will be perfect and complete, needing nothing.
—James 1:2–4

chapter 28

Fearfully and Wonderfully Made

The emotion of the previous two months only intensified the day after our twins were born. Early that day we announced and celebrated their names: Kristen and Jordan.

Later that morning I realized for the first time since November that there were no longer any restrictions. I was free to jump out of bed and walk down the hall, get a shower, or go to the cafeteria. But instead of racing down to the solarium, the nurse steadied me as I tried without success to stand by the bed. Almost two months of not moving my legs or flexing my toes had resulted in severe muscle atrophy. Who knew? Everything waist down felt and acted like Jell-O. So back into the bed I fell and sulked in a pool of self-pity.

The nurse informed us that I would require a wheelchair for the next few weeks. Physical therapists would work with me to get me back on my feet, but the process would take months. Norm was told he may have to carry me up and down steps when we got home. I'm not sure why we hadn't figured this issue out before. Why had no one prepared us for that tidbit of news? I felt like I had been kicked in the gut. But there it was, and we had three children who needed our immediate love and attention, so my lack of legs became the least of my worries.

We were ushered into a conference room where the doctors explained the bad news as they clicked the light so Norm and I could view the X-rays.

"Your son has a hardening of the lungs. See these black areas? It's called hyaline membrane disease. Sometimes we refer to it as infant respiratory distress syndrome. It's often fatal," they said, as if teaching a class.

They told us it was a condition in which the lungs hadn't developed properly in utero and had formed a hardened lining. We learned it wasn't uncommon with premature babies, especially second-born twin boys. None of his doctors expected him to live through the first couple of days.

Then after what seemed like forever, Norm and I were finally taken into the neonatal intensive care unit (NICU) to meet our babies. Our visit was short because of all the tubes, wires, and procedures still being performed. No words would come when I finally got to see and touch them for the first time. Those endless days and weeks of lying still in a darkened room had melted into a recent memory when I rolled through that door into the NICU and was greeted by computer created banners. They said "Welcome, Jordan and Kristen!" Prominently displayed across the back wall, it felt like the whole hospital was cheering for us.

So tiny and frail, just over four pounds, I remember thinking when I saw the translucence of Jordan's skin. *This was way too early, little one*, I thought as I tried to find a place on his face that wasn't covered by a tube. He was intubated, and it seemed his every short, labored breath was a struggle as he lay on his Sherpa under the bright lights of his incubator. Every new technology was being used in an effort to keep this tiny newborn, whose life hung in the balance, alive.

For some reason Kristen was on the other side of the room. I think she had graduated to the less critical area. One NICU nurse told me, "Kristen is a feisty one. She's a fighter, and that's a real advantage for preemies. We've already switched her to room air, so I believe she's going to continue to improve." That was the second bit of good news I can recall since their birth. We sent out a call for prayer to all our friends and family as we sat and prayed, feeling otherwise helpless. We stood on the promise, "The earnest prayer of a righteous person has great power and produces wonderful results." (James 5:16)

Jordan defied every prediction. Surviving those first few hours had been critical. To everyone's surprise, the hours clicked off and became one critical milestone after another. Soon we were allowed to sit with both babies in the NICU as often as we wanted. Believing our touch and presence were crucial to their survival, Norm and I tag-teamed with each baby so they could hear our voices, feel our touch, and bond with both of us as much as possible. Brandon usually came with Norm so he could talk, read books, and play with his new brother and sister, whom he called Seth and Lil Soul. He was as proud, vocal, and proactive as we were. Now that our family was together, none of us seemed eager to leave each other. Plus, Brandon had a lot of mommy time to catch up on.

I wanted to nurse our twins believing it would give them the best chance for a healthy future. That meant using a breast pump because they were too weak to nurse at the beginning. We did all we could to create the healthiest start possible under the circumstances. One or the other of us sat with our arm through the hole in Jordan's incubator stroking the few square inches of exposed face or arm that didn't have a tube or a wire over it. Hour after hour we told both babies stories, talked softly, and sang to them.

Everyone on the medical team marveled at how Jordan began to fight and improve seemingly by the day. Within that first week, the nurses put brother and sister in the same incubator so they could communicate. Something powerful happened. Jordan gained alertness and strength exponentially after his womb mate returned.

Though still in critical condition, he grew stronger by the day. Life is a beautiful gift. We never took it lightly. By the end of the first week they brought Kristen to my room so I could keep her with me skin to skin. The technique was called "kangarooing" and had proved to give newborns an advantage in mental, emotional, and physical development. A few days later, Jordan got to accompany his sister for the kangaroo therapy. So tiny and frail after having lost some of their birth weight, they felt like hairless squirrels snuggled on my chest.

Day after day Jordan dumbfounded his doctors. Both of them surpassed all expectations of the experts. Our twins were chosen as the March of Dimes babies that year because of their remarkable recovery due in part to the cutting-edge technology and skillful care of the medical staff at Missoula Community Hospital. They were featured in the Missoula newspapers and were famous for a short Montana minute.

After just over two weeks in the NICU, we were allowed to bring them home with monitors for their hearts. That decision to shorten our predicted stay was a miracle in itself. The doctors told us they had made that decision based on the trust we had built in the personal care of our children.

There were challenges to that first year with pre-mature twins. Going from one child to three in one fell swoop was something no book could have prepared us for. Because we needed a support group, we joined Missoula Mothers of Multiples. The friends we made there became an invaluable community of families who understood our challenges and helped us navigate our new world. Being together each week with other parents of multiples served to give us encouragement and weekly doses of much-needed sanity. Hearing from moms and dads, many of whom had more children than we did, offered different perspectives and helped us not to become isolated. That year our chapter put together a cookbook with unique recipes, which I still use decades later.

I learned to walk again after a few months of physical therapy, and the best part was that Norm didn't have to carry me up and down the stairs any longer. Our waterbed proved to be a nursing nightmare because it seemed I was always feeding one baby or the other. Norm cut a notch in the wooden frame so I could get in and out more easily. No, let's be honest. One actually rolls out of a waterbed!

Their recovery really was a miracle. Their first three years were something of a blur. But the twins made it with flying colors despite every professional prediction. They developed their own unique personalities and separate interests. Despite being twins, they turned out to be polar opposites in almost every way.

Kristen was the serious, gentle, quiet flower who obeyed quickly and almost never caused a ripple or required correction. Jordan, our hilariously funny clown, was always into, under, on top of, or inside something dangerous or off limits, keeping his parents ever on their toes. From the first year, they each had an insatiable curiosity and loved discovering life firsthand. Both proved to be natural athletes and loved sports and music with a passion.

Jordan drummed on everything that didn't walk away and a few things that did. A naturally gifted musician, he played the guitar and piano with trademark flare. Kristen picked up a violin when she was five. Her teacher declared her gifted, but she soon switched her interest to piano and developed a musical gift that has made our hearts sing for almost twenty years.

Perhaps because she had those early challenges, she is tenacious like flint, patient, gracious, and tenderhearted. Loving God and others with abandon, she is a loyal, attentive friend. Kristen has always been a self-motivated and brilliant student. Reading at the speed of light, she devours books and her college studies almost effortlessly. Since she was quite the natural athlete, basketball, soccer, and volleyball were her sports interests, and all of us screamed till our voices were gone at her tournaments and games for more years than I can count.

From childhood Jordan has kept us all in stitches and brought a joy to my heart I cannot explain. He and his big brother quickly became best buddies. Jordan thought Brandon was Superman and shadowed his every move. Naturally athletic, Jordan excelled in sports, playing baseball, soccer, basketball, and Ultimate Frisbee. He looked at each game as though the championship were always on the line.

A straight shooter and deep thinker, Jordan was our child who, when we were homeschooling, would hear the story or discussion and come up with the bottom line. "So basically you're saying he was an evil, lying tyrant," he would say bluntly. Or he would look up from his constantly drumming finger on the table to ask the one question everyone else wished he or she had thought of. Opposite but inseparable, he and Kristen even chose to attend the same college.

Today Jordan and Norm are partnering to build a family

business. Jordan's heart for God is obvious. Along with his music, he passionately pours his life into others. As a drummer he helps lead worship and mentors high school students through an organization called Young Life.

Kristen invests her life in the youth at our church and is finishing her business communications degree. She works at a locally owned business. One of the most pure-hearted, honest people I know, she continues to bring life, gentleness, goodness, and light wherever she goes.

For you created my inmost being;
you knit me together in my mother's womb.
I praise you because I am fearfully and wonderfully made;
your works are wonderful,
I know that full well.
My frame was not hidden from you
when I was made in the secret place,
when I was woven together in the depths of the earth.
Your eyes saw my unformed body;
all the days ordained for me were written in your book
before one of them came to be.

—Psalm 139:13–16

chapter 29

Kamikaze Memories

We had heard the statistics of people getting divorced after tragedies with children. For us the losses, stresses from all the moves, and stays in the hospital drew us closer and gave us even more reasons to love, respect, and honor one another. All those trials helped us grow in new ways and built new layers into the strata of our relationship. Instead of driving us apart, the trials acted like glue. They cemented us to each other and made us honest brokers to our promises for better or for worse, in sickness and in health. Through the wear, we were becoming real.

After the twins were a few months old, our work picked back up, and the little group of college students grew in numbers and in their thirst to know God. Spending time with the remarkable young women in our ministry, leading them through the Bible, and listening to their struggles over coffee or lunch were just a few of my daily joys.

Our door was always open, and some kind of better-than-cafeteria food was in the oven or simmering in a stockpot for the singles and groups who now dropped in to just hang out and love on our kids. Babysitters were never a problem in those days, and date nights actually became more routine.

Weekend ski trips to Big Sky, week-long retreats to Bozeman or Flathead Lake, Bible studies, pizza, spaghetti, or game nights, hayrides, cookouts (undeterred by the freezing temperatures), and much more filled our days with students. And our kids loved every crazy minute of it. In those years our days were filled with one drama, adventure, mystery, or side-splitting laugh after the next.

One day I remember above the rest. We had just moved to a house on a golf course, which we referred to as our "mansion on a hilltop." It was one of those signature Montana winter afternoons. A few inches of new snow sparkled across the golf course. Often called the hub of five valleys, the view from our backyard was of the spectacular convergence of the snow-covered Bitterroot, Sapphire, Garnet, and Rattlesnake Mountains, along with the Reservation Divide. It was no wonder the students hung out at our house so much. The million-dollar view kept calling them back for more. And from the top of the rolling fairway, with built-in moguls and long runs, it looked a little like the view from a ski lift in Aspen.

Norm had built a sled using an old pair of snow skis for runners. Sturdy and built for speed, that thing was the boss at about five feet long and thirty inches wide. Brandon helped his daddy wax the runners that morning, and the five of us planned for a fun day of snow-suiting on the slopes surrounding the house.

Having invited a group of students over to eat lunch and enjoy the day with us, Norm couldn't help but share a few stories featuring jumps and speeds made the previous week on his newly crafted flying machine. Those were all it took.

Before we knew it, the students had taken a couple of runs down the golf course and could be heard coming back up the hill, panting and out of breath, bragging of warp speed and daring feats aboard our now lightning-fast racer. Each trip down the course seemed to gain a student or two in the combinations with Brandon always somewhere in the mix.

The final run of the day was announced. We noticed the students piled one on top of the other like a stack of pancakes. Each peered downhill eagerly determined to set the day's record. Something ominous hovered in the air.

"Okay, I think there are too many of you on that thing this time," Norm protested needlessly since they had already shoved off. Sitting this one out, Brandon stood like a puffy statue at his daddy's side, looking on with awe and envy.

Down the mountain the neon pile of nylon flew, and as they approached that second mogul on which the sled normally got the best air and distance, they indeed got off the ground because we could see the light beneath them. But as they came down, the sled hit the ground and splintered into what must have been a zillion pieces all over the sixteenth green of that pristine golf course turned winter Olympics stadium. It was a story that grew more legendary and daring by the week and also by who was telling it.

Many of those students came to know the love and redemption of Christ for themselves during our years there at the University of Montana. Like all of us, they had been thirsty for truth in a world of relativity. They were looking for genuine relationships in the futility and emptiness of their hook-up facades. Some had known about God but realized their knowledge had been like knowing about Abraham Lincoln, Aristotle, or Elvis Presley. They knew a lot of facts but had never developed a personal relationship with any of them.

Norm had the privilege of baptizing some of them after their decisions of faith. It was such a privilege to walk with them and point them to the source of life, truth, and meaning that would affect the rest of their lives. Several still keep in touch and share pictures on Facebook of their families and achievements. All have changed their world in some way. God is faithful to use us, isn't He? He uses us right smack in the midst of our brokenness, pain, struggles, and questions—and in the simple joys that make life work. We are grateful that He uses crooked sticks to make straight lines.

I planted the seed in your hearts, and Apollos watered it, but it was God who made it grow. It's not important who does the planting, or who does the watering. What's important is that God makes the seed grow. The one who plants and the one who waters work together with the same purpose. And both will be rewarded for their own hard work. For we are both God's workers. And you are God's field. You are God's building.
—*1 Corinthians 3:6–9*

chapter 30

Sparrows and Springer Spaniels

Our golf course dream was short lived, because after only a year there, the house sold unexpectedly, and we had to move. God had always opened doors for us to have wonderfully spacious houses, but they were rentals, and they left us at the mercy of someone else's reasons for needing the house back.

This was our fourth move in three years, so we decided to buy a tiny fixer-upper instead of rolling the dice with landlords. With Norm's ever-growing remodeling skills and my love for decorating, we knew we could make some money whenever the time came to sell. All five of us lived in the unfinished basement with the mice while the hardwood floors were being refinished and the kitchen was gutted. With Jordan's asthma and all the dust, basement dwelling proved to be more than a challenge. We stuffed towels under all the doors and around the windows as best we could. The dust still won the day.

What proved a bigger problem was that we had given in to Brandon's incessant pleas for a puppy. For reasons unknown, we bought him a springer spaniel. Brandon proudly named his pup Sebastian. He was as black as coal with one white tuft on his chest, and he was softer than silk. His joyful antics and bounding, gracious kisses were beautiful gifts to us all. All except Jordan. After only a couple of months, it became apparent that he was highly allergic to dogs, especially to their saliva. Our first clues were the swollen eyes and lips and runny nose. At first we tried just keeping Jordan away most of the time. That didn't work. Then we tried keeping Sebastian outside and built him a sturdy house with a light bulb inside for warmth in the brutal cold. The doghouse worked for a while, but had its own set of reasons why it wouldn't fix things long term.

With each passing day, Brandon's heart bonded more with his dog, and truthfully everyone else bonded with the dog too. But after the umpteenth visit to the doctor for Jordan's allergies and his asthma kicking into high gear too often, we came to the painful realization that there was only one answer. Still holding onto hope, Brandon believed there must be a better solution, which would become apparent tomorrow. But though reluctant, in the end he saw his brother in swollen misery often enough to relent to the obvious. In late spring Norm and I made the decision that it was time to find Sebastian another home.

Norm put an ad in the *Missoulian,* and we prayed for the right person or family who would love him as much as we did. Within a day or two, we got a call from a university student who was heading home to help her parents with their ranch.

"My mom has cancer, so I will not be returning to the U. I want to come see him right now, if possible, because I am leaving town later this afternoon. But he sounds just perfect. Let me assure you, he would have lots of room to run on our ranch. It would also be great for my mom to have a dog around," she said as I held the phone, trying to give a wise reason why it wouldn't work.

The problem was that Norm and Brandon had gone to run errands, and I had no idea when they would return. Reasoning that it might be best if Brandon didn't have to be there to watch his dog go and that she might not even like the dog after all, I agreed to let her come and meet Sebastian.

In no time her packed-to-the-gills hatchback pulled up and parked on the street. Energy and confidence exuded from this girl as she bounded across the yard and onto the front porch. Sebastian met her at the door with matching enthusiasm. I witnessed an instant connection between dog and girl as she quickly got down on his level, hardly noticing the rest of us gathering around. What wasn't to love? The world's sweetest springer spaniel meets cute blonde coed with lots of words and dog-charmer magnetism.

We chatted a bit about the U, her mom, and her reasons for leaving school. Then after only about fifteen minutes, she blurted, "Oh, I love him! He's just what I wanted" while rubbing his ears and encouraging his licking and wiggling in the living room. "So, I'll take him now, if it's okay."

"Right now?" I repeated as if I hadn't already known what she would want to do.

Hemming and hawing for what seemed like way too long, I came to what I thought was a well-reasoned decision. "Well … then … let me get his things if you're leaving later today." I explained a little about our situation, and she expressed how difficult the decision must have been for all of us.

As soon as Sebastian's silhouette, perched up on her front seat, was out of sight, I knew I had made the worst decision of my almost five-year parenting career. I cried, stewed, prayed for mercy and forgiveness, and tried to keep busy as Jordan and Kristen played with their Duplos, oblivious to my tortured state of mind and breaking heart.

I was a total wreck when I finally heard Norm and Brandon come in the back door, chattering and laughing about their day. I met them and explained what had happened as gently as possible. As I spoke, Brandon did exactly what I had expected. He came unglued. For the first time in his five-year-old life, he was unable to control himself or his emotions. He screamed for his dog as he ran through the house, heartbroken and angry at not being able to say his proper goodbyes. I was almost as upset and angry with myself as he was with me.

When he finally calmed down enough to hear me, I remember getting down on my knees in front of him and saying through my tears, "Brandon, I am so sorry for letting your dog go without you being here. You have every right to be this angry with me. It was the wrong decision. I knew the minute he left that I had made a really bad choice. Honey, I will go over to the university right now, get Sebastian, and I will bring him home for you to be able to say goodbye. Okay?"

"Okay, Mommy" was about all he could manage through his sobs. We all prayed a quick prayer for Brandon and for me to find the pup before they left town.

With that I was off on a dog-finding mission. It was my own "mission impossible."

What had I just done? There was one small problem. I really had no idea where our cute coed lived on that massive campus. I didn't even know whether or not she was still in town. I searched my brain for any clues in our conversations as my car made one turn after the next toward the U of M campus. I remembered her talking about housemates. And she talked about taking her things down the steps to load her car, so I surmised she lived in a house of some sort with steps. Well, that certainly narrowed it down. Like many colleges, this one was surrounded by block after city bock of wonderful, old homes. Many of them had been painted white and turned into student housing or rentals.

I canvased one street after another, looking for her silver-tone hatchback or for someone sitting on a porch with a dog. A needle in a haystack is an understatement of what I was hoping to do. The stars would have to align at just the right moment, and I was feeling desperate and foolhardy as I rode, prayed, and scanned.

"Oh, Lord, please help me to find Sebastian. I know I really messed everything up. Will You show me where that dog is? I know you see the sparrow when he falls. I know You know where our dog is. Help me to find him," I prayed as I drove and searched both sides of the street.

Like a cop car searching for a burglar, I combed one block and then the next, methodically crawling along for what seemed like hours. All the streets and parallel- parked compact cars, sitting lazily in front of old fixer-uppers, all began to look the same.

"Haven't I been down this street before? Why didn't I write down the street names? What if she always parks in the back? Was that

187

her car? What if she had errands to run first and I miss her by ten minutes?" Each question haunted me more than the one before it.

I knew time wasn't on my side. I turned to begin the next block when I had the distinct prompting to comb back down a street I had already covered a couple of times.

"Really? I have been down that street more than once, and absolutely nothing was going on. There were no dogs anywhere," I said half aloud. But the prompting wouldn't let go.

Almost robotically, I turned around and retraced my path one more time, feeling a bit neurotic. Then, lo and behold, in the middle of the block, I looked up on the porch of a house I distinctly recalled seeing a few minutes before. Sitting there without a care in the world was the elusive coed, who was stroking the shiny coat of her new dog. I pulled over, got out, and called, "Hey, I can't believe I found you! My son was so heartbroken over not getting to see his dog off that I promised him I would search for you guys. Can I come up for a minute?"

"Sure," she said without flinching. She had just gone outside to relax on the porch for the final time after packing the last of her things. I had missed her earlier by only a couple of minutes.

She was gracious enough to let me take Sebastian back home for the proper goodbyes upon my promise to have him back before the time she planned to leave.

When I drove up to the house, Brandon and everyone else came bounding out with yelps of surprise and gratitude at the sight of Sebastian in the car.

The sloppy reunion between dog and boy made time stand still. Norm and I put our arms around each other as we stood in the yard, awed by the sight. I quietly told him the story as we watched Brandon romp with his dog one last time. Truthfully, the whole thing sounded like a fairy tale, even to me. That final dance around the house and on the ground was filled with joy, agony, dread, gratitude, and happy grief for us all.

Standing there on Wapikiya Drive at the end of that day under a vast Montana sky, I felt so small yet so seen and heard by the God of the universe. Who were we that He should notice? The same God who had created the stars and formed the snow-capped mountains all around us cared about little boys' broken hearts. And that same God cared enough to whisper into a mother's desperate quest to correct her wrong on behalf of her son. That day there were both whispers in my joys and shouts in my pain.

Thankfully, there would be other amazing stories of pets in our lives. But this one wrought a unique lesson of faith we all still draw from with pricks of humility and notes of wonder at the goodness and redemption of God. It was one more whisper of love and grace I will never forget.

"Look at the birds. They don't plant or harvest or store food in barns, for your heavenly Father feeds them. And aren't you far more valuable to him than they are? "Can all your worries add a single moment to your life? And why worry about your clothing? Look at the lilies of the field and how they grow. They don't work or make their clothing, yet Solomon in all his glory was not dressed as beautifully as they are. And if God cares so wonderfully for wildflowers that are here today and thrown into the fire tomorrow, he will certainly care for you. Why do you have so little faith? So don't worry about these things, saying, 'What will we eat? What will we drink? What will we wear?' These things dominate the thoughts of unbelievers, but your heavenly Father already knows all your needs. Seek the Kingdom of God above all else, and live righteously, and he will give you everything you need."

—Matthew 6:26–33

chapter 31

We Live by Faith, Not by Sight

Missoula held rich experiences for our active family of five. There were trips to Flathead Lake, Glacier, and Yellowstone National Parks. Our friends Chris and Sue from Fort Worth were doing campus ministry in Bozeman. Their kids were similar ages to ours, and that meant many treks to and from their house. Weekend trips to Livingston, ski retreats at Big Sky, hayrides in the snow, trips over Lolo Pass, and a hundred other breathtaking events fill our memories. There were church picnics, nights spent marveling at the northern lights, and moments to enjoy every little hole-in-the-wall eatery in Missoula.

But we also encountered some devastating blows in those three years. The hospital bills alone seemed insurmountable. Then there were expenses from when I totaled our van in a collision near the university. With three kids strapped into their car seats, we flew into the air and flipped onto its top. The twins were only a couple of months old at the time. I literally saw the pebbles and the lines on the pavement through the windshield, inches from my face, as we slid around in an intersection after dropping Norm off at the airport. Thankfully, no one had more than a few cuts, bruises, and whiplash.

About three months following the twins' delivery, my health spiraled. I developed unrelenting muscle and joint pain, headaches, and depression. Norm worked triple duty as caregiver, dad, and campus minister. His patience and ability to deal effectively with all the stress grew thinner as the months passed. He had been my strong, resilient rock through all those ups and downs and days I couldn't get out of bed. Now I worried that his breaking point was near. Both of us found ourselves weary from the emotional roller coaster we had been on for several years. People who knew us well counseled us to take a break from ministry and just focus on our family and recovering my declining health. They suggested moving closer to our families for help and support both physically and emotionally. We listened.

After three years in Missoula, we made the decision to take a sabbatical. For two to three years we would go somewhere to rest. After considering our options, we chose to move to the mountains of North Carolina near Asheville. That would locate us just over an hour from each of our families. It seemed too good to be true. For years, as we traveled home from Nashville or Fort Worth through the Blue Ridge Mountains, I commented on the beauty and special feel of the Asheville area. It seemed like a pipe dream to actually get to live there.

We moved in with my parents until we found a cute rental near the airport. We had been in Asheville only a couple months when we got the news that another baby was on the way. We were guardedly optimistic through the first trimester. Feeling better as the weeks became three months, we shared the news with friends and family who rejoiced with us. Our parents seemed excited that they would have a new grandbaby to dote on who wasn't a thousand miles away. But as I entered the second trimester, I suffered another miscarriage. It was far worse than the one I had suffered in Fort Worth. Norm had found me unconscious on the floor and called 911. In the ambulance I vaguely remember them discussing that I had lost over half my blood in the hemorrhage. Another miscarriage and subsequent surgery left us both emotionally and physically weary.

Though we weren't able to verbalize it all then, we were learning that grief points us to a deeper truth. The pain of grief drives us to Jesus first of all. It also calls us to understand that we weren't made to experience death. Death wasn't part of God's perfect place with his perfect relationship between mankind and Himself. We weren't made to deal daily with the ravages and pain of sin and depravity. We were made for heaven. That is our eternal home. All the brokenness, separation, and effects of sin we grapple with here serve to remind us of the hope we have in Christ alone. They remind us that our hope isn't in circumstances, in living the blessed life, or in whether events turn out as we expect. Our hope is in the changeless One. Nothing else. We sensed God was showing us glimpses of all that. Though we clung tightly, He was also prying our fingers off the things of this world and setting our sights on things we couldn't see.

Even with our knowledge of scripture and our faith in God, we still deeply grieved the loss of three children. Personally, I struggled not to let those losses become my focal point and take me under. Almost daily, fear and doubt clouded my mind and threatened to quench my joy. There were days I couldn't get my head up. But we had been blessed with three amazing gifts from God. By God's grace, I could focus there. So with open-handed trust in the fact that God knew and we did not, Norm and I did the only thing we could do at that time. We did the next thing. And it made sense to us that the next thing was to quickly and finally come to terms with the obvious. All the evidence and the pain of the past few years pointed in one direction. Our family was now complete. Our quiver was full. After all, I was almost thirty-seven.

For we know that when this earthly tent we live in is taken down (that is, when we die and leave this earthly body), we will have a house in heaven, an eternal body made for us by God himself and not by human hands...For we live by believing and not by seeing.
—*2 Corinthians 5:1, 7*

chapter 32

Higher and Wiser

God's ways are infinitely higher and wiser than ours. That is one of those mysteries I can never get my mind around. I decided as a child that I just needed to accept it and move on. Perhaps that was faith. Such was my mindset when we moved back to the mountainous beauty of North Carolina. Enjoying all the advantages of living closer to both our families, we reveled in the lush scenery surrounding us. We had always viewed that area as a little taste of heaven where the Blue Ridge Mountains met the The Great Smokies. I took no moment for granted, and every breath seemed like a personalized gift just for me. If only for a little while, I was home.

Biking, hiking, and exploring the trails and waterfalls of western North Carolina with three bundles of endless curiosity filled our weekends. Just the sight of our three kids piling out of the van and scrambling for time with their Mawmaw and Pawpaw, or Grandmommy and Granddaddy, was always worth the price of admission. Life was good.

Jordan and Kristen turned three, and Brandon entered first grade the year we moved to Fletcher. Living near the airport, we grew used to stopping in mid-conversation as we listened and learned the differences between the sounds of takeoff and landing patterns; or of turbo props and jets. Most of my days found me surrounded by three curious bundles of energy, messy projects of some kind, and stacks of books. We took field trips to sheep farms, orchards, and nature centers. The kids played outside for hours, building Daniel Boone forts and Ninja Turtle kingdoms in the backyard with scraps of whatever they could piece together. Homemade superhero capes gave them courage and reasons for daring leaps off our back deck. Makeshift graveyards supplied holy ground for captured critters to receive a proper burial when the time inevitably came.

As summer ended and the leaves gained tinges of color, I began noticing a thick sensation that started at the back of my throat and moved all the way to my knees in the mornings. Lingering into the afternoon and striking in waves, I knew that feeling all too well. Whether you call it feeling green, morning sickness, or nausea; it could mean only one thing. Even after seeing the positive result from the home pregnancy test, I kept my news private for days. When I finally mustered the nerve to share my secret with Norm, we agreed to tell absolutely no one.

Ironically, within a few weeks though, Norm and I began bantering the possibility of choosing a home birth. It was all in good fun at first. Several friends in the area had gone that route and had glowing stories. Home births were in. I know what you're thinking. But after several discussions, we agreed that if I carried this baby to term, we wanted a quieter experience than all the others. Maybe it was a way to focus on the positive. Perhaps it was a nostalgic decision because of the contrasting memories of hospitals with incessant beeping, lights, and medical mayhem. Or maybe we had become a little rebellious of normal procedures and wanted a totally different, more serene set of memories. More than likely, though, it was just the weirdness in the Asheville air that had gotten to us.

We chose the one person all our close friends had recommended. Her experience and expertise impressed us having delivered over two thousand babies. Hiring an experienced midwife turned out to be a greater asset and truer gift than we ever imagined.

Then, as if on cue, evidence of another miscarriage began around eight weeks. What began as daily spotting became more severe over the next two weeks. Our midwife, DeeEtte, told us we were most likely losing our surprise baby. All we could do now was pray and wait.

The bleeding continued unabated. But despite all our expectations, it became obvious due to my ever-expanding waistline that our baby was growing.

Puzzled by what was really going on, she ordered an ultrasound around the sixteenth week. The pictures revealed a large hematoma that had ruptured alongside the placenta. It appeared the hematoma had almost depleted itself at that point. The doctors assured us that the sack was the culprit for the bleeding for the past two months. They felt certain it would taper off completely within a couple more weeks.

Our relief came not only because we discovered the reason for the bleeding, but because the pictures revealed a perfectly healthy baby girl. Relief and joy filled our car as we drove home. Within a couple of weeks, all bleeding stopped as the doctors had predicted. With three months to go before the due date, we could finally begin preparations for our newest addition.

About a week before her due date, I noticed a sharp decrease in the baby's movement. Her kicks, which had been quite strong for weeks, had grown steadily weaker. Those factors spurred in me a foreboding that wouldn't go away. We had lost Justin at almost the same time of year. Memories of that loss raced in all too willingly. At first I chalked my fears up to the fact that most pregnant women worry needlessly and tend to get a little edgy in the last couple of weeks. Hormones rage. But despite that self-awareness and acknowledgment of my usual tendency toward fear, the uneasy feelings intensified.

That same week Norm was doing some barter painting for DeeEtte and her husband. He told her what was going on. Being a woman who believed in the power of prayer, she began to pray. She called and asked me to pray for an hour, after which we would compare notes. Grateful for the sanity check, I agreed to pray. After an hour of asking God for guidance, I knew it was time. "I believe we need to move this birth along. How quickly can you get here?" I asked her.

"My things are already in the car. I'll be there in less than two hours," she said with a seriousness I knew as her midwife voice. I could almost see her heading out the door, oxygen tank and medical bag in hand.

I followed instructions and kick-started my labor with a few tricks of the trade, beginning by throwing back that nasty cherry-flavored castor oil. Blaagh! We were full speed ahead just after noon on that brilliant day in May when DeeEtte arrived at our little spit-level on Wildwood Lane.

The windows were open, welcoming the fragrant North Carolina spring into every room and filling our bedroom turned birthing center with its freshness. As the sterile utensils were laid out neatly in the tray on the dresser, the oxygen tank, epidural, and various other necessities were stationed like minutemen at the ready.

This was a day we thought might never come, a day we had bathed in prayer. "Are you sure you brought the epidural? I'm just checking," I said as I paced the floors.

"I came well equipped. The epidural is right here," DeeEtte reassured me.

I thought of how grateful I was for Scott and Corinne Holmquist, generous friends from church who had volunteered to take our three older children to their home for the big day. What would we do without the gift of friends?

My labor began in earnest at around three that afternoon with harder contractions quickly becoming closer together. Since we had chosen that I would labor in water, I drew the warmest tub possible. But my plans for a water labor were short lived as the contractions became so intense and frequent that the midwife needed to check my progress. Transition hit faster and with more intensity than with my others. I was on the verge of losing the control I had worked hard to maintain. "I think I need that epidural now," I pleaded, my voice and body noticeably shivering.

Everything from there went quickly. The next contraction did its work. Next thing I knew, everything changed with my midwife's tone. "Denise, you just went from five to ten centimeters with that last contraction. You're ready to push. Listen to me. There's not going to be time for the epidural. You need to push. Now." Norm stood aside, and her focused work continued undisturbed.

I feel certain that my final primal scream streaming from the open windows of our bedroom/birthing center lingered hauntingly in the air of our neighborhood for hours.

One and done. At 5:16 p.m., our fourth baby, Kathryn, made her journey from warm, cozy, and tucked in to cold, bright, and spacious. No wonder babies flail their arms, close their eyes, and cry like that.

"Hmmm, there it is. Look … There's the reason you felt prompted that today was the day," came DeeEtte's confident, assuring words as she skillfully worked to unwind the umbilical cord. She expertly drew the baby from my womb and began preparing the beautifully new, flailing treasure for my impatient arms.

"She wouldn't have made it another day. God just prompted our hearts this morning." She continued without missing a beat. "Thank God you were attentive. The cord was wrapped through the legs and around her neck. It was beginning to restrict oxygen. That's probably why her movement had slowed this week. See right here." Our midwife spoke calmly as she pointed out the obvious twisted, dark kink in the cord. Then she showed us the depleted hematoma sack that had been the culprit for all those weeks of mysterious bleeding. Her knowing tone helped me understand why we had chosen this unconventional route.

As I sighed a prayer of thanksgiving and reached to hold my little seven-pound, two-ounce miracle, straight from the hands of God, I felt the exhausted, euphoric joy that has been the bonding language of women for millennia. Wonder. No words. Only tears of unspeakable gratitude for things mere verbiage would have cheapened.

All the official paperwork was soon completed in silence as each sound in the room now had a different, more distant tone, like respectful shadows keeping to themselves. While little ink footprints were imprinted on ecru paper, measurements were made, and Kathryn showed off her healthy lungs. Norm made the necessary proud papa phone calls. I rested, reveling in the relief and sweet mystery of it all.

Within the next hour or so, Scott peeked into the room with

grins and kind words of congratulations. We gathered our three other children onto the bed with us, and there was a joyful cacophony as our now-completed family became acquainted with its newest member.

"Can I touch her?"

"What's her name?"

"How does she eat?"

"Can she see us?"

"Can you show me how to hold her?"

"She's so little."

"Look, Mommy, she's got my finger."

"When can we give her a bath?"

Their questions spun off each other in newfound curiosity. They loved her at once.

Norm and DeeEtte filled a little, white plastic bathtub half full with warm water and put it beside me on the bed for our new addition's first bath. Taking turns, Brandon, Kristen, and Jordan all tenderly and proudly helped DeeEtte keep the water out of her eyes as they washed, dried, and swaddled their new little sister. Norm and I looked on with awe at the goodness, wisdom, and redemption on grand display on this, our own private day of miracles.

God writes our stories differently than we would have chosen, doesn't He? For each of our children, God has often allowed me to sense His steady, faithful pen. Like each of them, Kathryn could write her own book. But there is a bit more I will share here about the fourth and final arrow in our quiver.

At her eight-month checkup, her doctor discovered she had severe intoeing and rotated hips. The rotation was so severe the doctors told us she would probably never be able to run. And if she did, it wouldn't be without difficulty. Norm and I were all ears as to what we could do for her.

She was soon referred to Shriner's Hospital and, along with Kristen, was seen there for several years. The doctors and nurses at Shriner's were amazingly kind and helpful in her treatment. For years, we did various therapies and nightly massages to encourage her bones to reshape in the opposite direction. For two years she had to wear special shoes with steel sides on the wrong feet as part of the therapy. Perhaps that's why in addition to cheering wildly, I also shed my share of grateful tears while watching her steal the ball to make a breakaway layup at her basketball games or dive and dig on the gym floor during volleyball tournaments.

I used to call her my "girl of a thousand faces." When she was about two, Kathryn would sit on my lap, facing me, and make me cackle aloud with one silly face after another. Turning her head down and away from me, she reemerged with hair swirling wildly, producing yet another cross-eyed or tongue-twisted contortion to delight my soul. On days when I was sad or stressed out, her funny face game turned my day around.

Kathryn has a musical gift. As a toddler she made up the most amazing songs to accompany every ordinary situation. Sometimes I wondered whether she had heard that one on the radio. But they were her originals. Making our whole house sing, Kathryn became notorious for creating lyrics and a tune to the most menial task. If you stopped to listen, you could usually hear her off in another room, singing to herself about the rain, her puppy, or her friend who was coming over to play.

Kathryn was a nonreader at nine. Everything was uphill. "Why can't I read like Kristen, Mommy?" The tears welled as she stared blankly at the pages of her reader while Kristen sat devouring the last chapter of *The Lion, the Witch, and the Wardrobe*.

In the first few years of school, because she was so smart and able to memorize quickly, Kathryn asked me to read a page to her, and she read it back. Her recollection echoed what I had read almost verbatim. That went on for months. Norm and I thought she just had more trouble reading than our other children. But her problem didn't improve.

Even after two years of private tutoring with a reading specialist, she made no measurable improvements. Then after a series of tests, we got the diagnosis.

"Is she dyslexic?" came the incredulous reply from the master teacher when I voiced my suspicions. "She is probably one of the most highly dyslexic children I have ever tested," she stated as she sat across the table from me.

"Does she see everything backwards?" was the only question I could stammer at first.

"Here, read these," she replied, reaching into her briefcase.

She held up for me a series of cards displaying bold symbols that were actually words written in Chinese.

"This is how she sees the flash cards you hold up for her. It's how the words and figures on a page often look to her," she explained. "It isn't that she sees them all backwards. She sees most everything differently than we do, like a foreign language. Your daughter will need to have tools to help her unscramble them and put words in correct order first of all. With proper tools and training, she can learn to read well. But it won't be quick or easy, for her, or for you."

Those were sobering yet musical words. We finally had some hooks to hang our questions on. But how and where to begin?

As her teachers, Norm and I would do whatever it took. We read, researched, and questioned. That summer we enrolled in classes to become certified to teach her using a curriculum we had discovered for children with dyslexia called Orton-Gillingham. It was just what the doctor ordered. Improvements were not immediate, but over months of teaching her to use the tools, she began to enjoy reading. Nothing came easily for Kathryn. To this day, listening and learning through books on CD are still her preference.

Just after learning she had dyslexia, Kathryn announced, "Mom, I think I want to take piano lessons like Jordan and Kristen. Could you see if Mrs. Collette will teach me?"

We discussed the extent of Kathryn's struggles with her piano teacher, but after Kathryn's second lesson, her teacher pulled me aside and confided, "I was amazed. Kathryn plays the notes perfectly … backwards. But she plays them with confidence!"

Having taught other children with learning difficulties, her teacher explained to me that the struggle Kathryn would have in reading and playing musical scores correctly would actually help her read everything else better. Mrs. Collette encouraged Kathryn to continue. Just like with all the other challenges, she would take that bull by the horns.

So after receiving her nine-year trophy in piano, you might imagine the reasons for my tears during that last recital. Who am I kidding? I was a mess from year one. But there was something special about her difficult senior recital piece, which she played with such quiet confidence and grace.

Just last week, I sank onto the sofa to relax as she played a hymn. "You make me nervous. I make more mistakes when you come in to listen," she said, not missing a beat.

"I just love hearing you play, sweetie. Pretend I'm not here," I said as I closed my eyes and soaked in the moment.

Gregarious, fun loving, adventurous, Kathryn is everyone's best friend. She, along with her siblings, has enjoyed swing and contra dancing for several years. I marvel as I watch their twirls, dips, and spins, whether across the Warren Wilson College dance floor or on our back deck, which was often strung with tiny Christmas lights for some special evening occasion.

Kathryn loves God deeply and serves people selflessly. Along with being "world's best nanny" to three beautiful little girls for the past eight years, she has her own business of organizing homes and offices. One of her God-given talents is creating order out of chaos. When I feel overwhelmed with an area of my house, I just say, "Kathryn, come give me thirty minutes and wave your magic wand."

Thirty minutes later, sweet serenity and order reign. Being the world's best nanny and having her organizing business have proved perfect jobs for putting herself through college.

For twenty-two years and counting, Kathryn has exemplified the beauty of joyful, tenacious courage and grace. Despite—and maybe because of—her many challenges, she has become a strong young woman with her own set of ever-growing gifts and passions. She is a bright spot in every room she enters.

Children are a gift from the Lord;
they are a reward from him.
Children born to a young man
are like arrows in a warrior's hands.
How joyful is the man whose quiver is full of them!
—Psalm 127:3–5

chapter 33

Living as Sons and Daughters

Those fifteen years culminated in a full quiver. God used it all—the joys, the intensity of our brokenness, the counseling, the conferences, the closed doors, our countless failures, the innumerable experiences of people walking alongside us, our love for each other, our love for God, and our losses and pain. Those were all gifts we didn't know how to value then.

Norm and I will celebrate our thirty-sixth anniversary this year. God continues to lead us deeper into His plan for our marriage. We sense we have just scratched the surface of what He has for us as we learn to hear and desire His voice above all others.

One of the places He has directed me recently is into the field of life coaching. As a marriage coach, I ask questions and operate in God-dependent curiosity. Jesus asked questions and told stories as a way to relate eternal principles and concepts to time-bound minds like mine. I am grateful He has honored our desire to always be learners.

As I study the stories in the Bible, I pause to ponder the questions. I am struck by how Jesus' questions raise our gaze. For example, they take our attention from the shame and nakedness of the woman caught in adultery and raise it to the fact that we are *all* sinners in need of redemption. God's stories point us away from lions, giants, armies, wind, and waves; and they cause us to see, hear, and worship God in the everydayness of life. Maybe that's their ultimate purpose.

In conclusion, I would like to share one more story about a time Norm asked important questions and the way God answered them. This event marked a significant turning point in the life of our family. It was another point of no return. God continues to whisper His faithfulness and shout His tenacious pursuit of us every time this story crosses my mind. With Norm's permission, I pull back one more curtain.

There was no doubt that our faith had been stretched over those first fifteen years. It had mostly been a gradual growth that was subtle and unnoticeable, like ships rising with the tide. Our marriage had seen beautiful highs. Like most people, we had also faced some seasons of gale-force winds. Those years had made us grateful for the ways God sustained us through circumstances that had often torn marriages apart.

When we moved from Montana to North Carolina, there was a change in my husband that impacted our family for years. Norm entered an isolating struggle that was unlike any of the ones we had weathered together. It revolved around two main areas of his life: his identity (who he was) and his calling or purpose (what he was meant to do). He had wrestled with questions before, but during those years he was asking, "Am I enough? Do I even have what it takes?"

Looking back, I realize there were many reasons that his self-doubt and anger had resurfaced and intensified: financial pressures, grief, loss of purpose, old patterns, shattered dreams, never-ending stress. For those and other reasons, he had hit his wall.

Because he and I dealt with intense emotion and crises so differently, we found ourselves at a loss, inept and unable to communicate effectively much of the time. The distance between us grew wider as the months became years. Norm's growing anger and controlling silence, along with my wounded, needy heart, self-preservation, and hypersensitivity to criticism, had met for yet another series of battles.

Even after knowing scripture and walking with God for as long as we had, we found ourselves trudging along without answers. We were running on empty and separately crying out to God for help. Our communication was often minimal at best.

We knew in our heads that looking to anything or anyone other than Jesus to meet our needs was a surefire recipe for disaster. We knew we were not enough. We both had verbalized that we didn't have what it took apart from God. But our head knowledge got stuck in the mud of our emotional brokenness during that long season of impasse. More often than we wanted to admit, we had allowed pride, performance-based acceptance, and rule keeping to reign supreme over relationships in our home. Everyone felt the tension. Norm's nonverbal disapproval communicated his unhappiness loudly too much of the time. Often our feet ached from the eggshells we found ourselves walking on.

The experience was reminiscent of the first year or so of our marriage; it felt like our now-bigger family had once again become that volcano with the lava of anger and fear flowing just beneath the surface. With Brandon being the eldest child, he and I felt it most. I tried to be the buffer for Daddy's anger and silence. I explained it away as his just having had another hard day. But more and more often, the kids and I found ourselves waiting for Daddy's next explosion followed by my subsequent tears as we fled to higher ground. There seemed to be no explanation and no end in sight. I had had just about enough. Norm and I were at loggerheads and decided to seek counseling to see whether we could unravel some of the mess. I was not hopeful.

At about that same time, some men from our church invited Norm to participate in a sixteen-week course called *Sonship*. It was an in-depth Bible study and had as its theme the truth that we *all* wake up every morning in desperate need of a Savior. Each week Norm was reminded of the reality that we are more stained, more broken, more sinful than we ever want to admit; but at the same time, we are more deeply loved than the human mind can comprehend. The gospel message was put simply and given time to sink in through stories of how we are sons, not orphans.

Grace at Christ's expense and God's deep love for us as His sons and daughters were the familiar themes Norm chewed on for four life-changing months. Love and grace. Grace and love. He began longing with renewed energy for the truths he was grasping anew to become a daily reality in his life. His sincere longing to see the gospel transform our home became evident.

We had just bought a little fixer-upper. Phase one of our remodel had been completed, and I was no longer washing dishes in the bathtub. Norm had installed white kitchen cabinets and a shiny white tile floor. They looked sharp against the kelly-green countertops.

Early one morning we were getting ready for our day. Norm finished his breakfast and was heading out to work in the yard. Seven-year-old Kristen came into the kitchen and was being her usual sweet, independent self as I scrambled some eggs. She reached into the fridge to get the juice. When she pulled it out, she realized it was full and heavier than anticipated. Almost in slow motion, dark purple splashed across the floor, all over herself, and up onto the lower cabinets, creating a grape-splendor contrast fit for a Bounty commercial.

Kristen's eyes filled with tears. She looked up at her daddy, horrified and expecting an angry lecture or reprimand. But almost as quickly as the plastic pitcher hit the floor, Norm fell to his knees and said, "It's okay, honey. I've done things much worse than this. And I do them all the time."

He scooped her up in his arms and held her as she cried. Then he said with a tenderness that came from a newly-carved place of grace and mercy, "Here, let's get some towels, and we'll clean this up together." I stood in tears of amazement at his response. By then everyone was in the kitchen, almost having fun while cleaning grape juice stains off white surfaces.

Norm did the heavy lifting that day and in the days and weeks following. His transformed heart was evident, not just with the cleanup but with asking forgiveness and doing his sincere efforts to make amends to all his children and me over time. God had radically changed Norm's heart through that long view of seeing himself as both a sinner and a grateful son of God.

He began making one God-directed hard pivot after another. With each choice, the atmosphere in our home became sweeter and more alive than I ever thought possible again. From that point forward, his tenacity toward loving his family better spurred transforming choices and changes in all of us. Because of the stark differences I witnessed in my husband, I enrolled in the course a few months later. God used it powerfully in my life as well.

I think that is the real trademark of a leader, not someone who always does it right, but someone who can detect when he's doing it wrong, repent, and do whatever it takes to correct it. I have seen Norm do the hard things more times now than I can count. He is the kind of good servant-leader others want to follow. He has earned widespread respect because of his strong but gentle spirit that was born in pain, loss, and the vulnerability of seeing his own sin first and foremost. Restoration and forgiveness draw us toward relationships. The gospel calls us to relate differently.

I am discovering that a gospel-centered marriage requires a radical commitment to love our spouses just as they are while at the same time longing for and holding a place for them to become all God created them to be. We are made to ever point each other in love not to what we are not yet, but to what by God's grace we someday will be. Daily we are learning to live now as though we are already home. Though we fail often and are always in process, we take great comfort in knowing we are being formed into His image.

God's calling to each of us as sons and daughters is a high calling. He calls us to be holy as He is holy and to know the truth to live with purpose and in freedom. The freedom of the cross. His invitation into His greater story is for our good and His glory. It is an eternal love story that beckons us to join in the beauty of His dance. But we must always factor in that we have an enemy, whose aim is to kill, steal, and destroy everything God has established. Our opponent's unrelenting goal is to thwart the purposes of God in and around us.

Like in the Garden of Eden, very often Satan accomplishes such devastation by twisting or distorting things, even the very words of God. "Did God really say …?" As liar-in-chief, Satan annihilates individuals, marriages, families, churches, businesses, relationships, and cultures. The world, the flesh and the devil make up the unholy trinity; a ruinous unity. The three, in reality, are defeated foes who have been given a short reign on the earth. Evidence of their effectiveness is all around us. It will not always be so.

For now, though, we live in enemy territory. Our world is not as it was intended. We will someday rejoice as Jesus, our risen Redeemer, steps onto the stage to restore all things. As our warrior King, He will then destroy all the works of the evil one. Until then, we both fight and trust with all the armor and courage God has afforded us through His Spirit, knowing God is ultimately in control. Sometimes we resist. Sometimes we flee. Sometimes we stand and fight. And whichever we are called to do at the moment, it is always with the knowledge that He who lives in us is greater than the one who is in the world (1 John 1:4).

I think often of that picture of Norm and his response to Kristen on his knees in our kitchen floor. He was identifying as a son of God. Norm in his humanness was stepping into his real identity in Christ as he lovingly held his child and helped her clean up the mess. It is a fitting picture of humankind. Norm's longing for true identity and his hope for better relationships with family were indicators that such things were possible.

Ultimately, Christians are called to be little christs. It is God, not us, who is the faithful One able to accomplish what He started. What a thought! Our longings to be all that He has called us to will be met only in part here. We get momentary tastes and dim glimpses of the real thing every now and then.

In *Mere Christianity*, C. S. Lewis talks about our desires and how God gives us deep longings and even pain to guide us and move us toward the goal. Perhaps that's what the whispers and shouts in each of our stories are really about. They are spoken to us by the One for whom we were made. He ever calls us higher up and further in. Lewis puts it like this:

The Christian says, "Creatures are not born with desires unless satisfaction for those desires exists. A baby feels hunger: well, there is such a thing as food. A duckling wants to swim: well, there is such a thing as water. Men feel sexual desire: well, there is such a thing as sex. If I find in myself a desire which no experience in this world can satisfy, the most probable explanation is that I was made for another world ... I must keep alive in myself a desire for my true country, which I shall not find till after death; I must never let it get snowed under or turned aside; I must make it the main object of life to press on to that other country and to help others do the same."

"My sheep listen to my voice; I know them, and they follow me. I give them eternal life, and they will never perish. No one can snatch them away from me, for my Father has given them to me, and he is more powerful than anyone else. No one can snatch them from the Father's hand."

—John 10:27–29

Epilogue

I wrote this a few months after our youngest, Kathryn, finished high school. It was during the time I was getting my certification to become a life coach and before I began writing this book. I was searching for what God might be saying in the midst of several wrenching transitions. I wanted to share this epilogue as an addition to *Whispers and Shouts* and as a brief summation of our homeschooling years.

It didn't really hit me until the day after Kathryn, our youngest daughter, graduated from high school. As I watched another graduation ceremony and viewed slide shows of friends with whom our children had grown up, I was overcome with the gut-wrenching realization that life as I had known it for twenty-two years was now ... over.

With that awareness came momentary panic, tears, and a flood of memories that drew me to a lonely place and threw me into a private depression, which took several weeks to work through and climb out of.

You see, for twenty-two precious years, my life had been built around the daily joys and challenges of homeschooling. In the early years, we worked on reading, simple math, writing, and grammar. Lesson plans were chock full of both the wonder and surprise of science experiments, such as mixing baking soda and vinegar to create active, oozing volcanoes; making bread and cookies fresh from the oven; acting out scenes in history with swords, shields, and crowns; and planting, tending, and enjoying the fruit of our backyard garden. My days often held challenges such as prying kids from treetops;

exploring sandy critter-filled creek beds; creating homemade forts; giving permission and space for hours of discovery in the woods, replete with caves, critters, and pockets full of rocks and acorns; and listening to what only nature might teach.

I remember lunchtime planning and sticky cleanup duty, chore charts, bug and leaf collections, and finger paintings and sketches downstairs in the art room. And I can still feel the constant challenges and daily drama of navigating four very different children's learning styles. Some of our most rewarding memories were the constant flow of friends coming over for game nights, family video nights, bonfires on the deck, weekend camping trips, or just to hang out at the Williams house.

We were always in the midst of reading a good book, rehearsing lines for the Christmas play, or encouraging the progress of year-end piano or violin recitals. We enjoyed field trips to the sheep farms, where we learned how wool becomes clothing, and to Carl Sandburg's house to visit the Connemara goats, where we had several years' worth of pictures made with scarecrows amid their yearly garden splendor.

Fun songs and bantering conversations filled our old conversion van as our family of six took several memory-laced cross-country trips to amazing places, such as the Alamo; the Grand Canyon; Pike's Peak and Estes Park; Mount Vernon; the Outer Banks and Kitty Hawk; Washington, DC; New Orleans; Old Williamsburg; and maybe a hundred other places. Each anticipated destination held education, fun facts, priceless family time, and lessons on how to navigate a thousand relationship challenges along the way.

"I call the back seat!"

"I get the top bunk."

"Who keeps using my toothbrush?"

"Mom, tell Jordan to stop punching me!"

"Jordaaan! Come away from that ledge! Didn't you read the 'Dangerous Drop Off/Stay Behind Barriers' signs? You are going to give your mama a heart attack."

And sports. Ah, yes, always sports, which are my go-to outlet, much preferred to shopping malls. First there was Little League, then baseball, soccer, basketball, volleyball, and Ultimate Frisbee. The most recent memories are of Kristen and Kathryn's basketball and volleyball years. I can vividly recall going on numerous raucous road trips to games and excitedly cheering at state championships till our voices were hoarse. Those memories silhouetted against the silent late-night drives home while we looked proudly over our shoulders at our sleeping champions in the seats behind us.

That part of our story has ended. What an incredible journey. What a privilege to have homeschooled four amazing gifts from God all these years and now to possess such a treasure trove of memories. From the time our children were little, I remember stooping down to put on their socks and shoes, and thinking that as parents, *We serve before kings and queens*. It is true.

Now, looking back, I realize that each day I had with my children, no matter how difficult, joyful, messy, or ordinary, was both a priceless gift and a worthwhile investment. I am reminded that by the grace of God that investment has yielded four uniquely gifted, surprisingly sane young men and women who now pursue their own dreams.

So, when the thought hit me that week of Kathryn's graduation that life as I had known it was over, I found myself feeling empty, alone, directionless, and depressed. It was a dark place I hadn't seen coming. And for several months, I didn't come up for air. But somehow right along with that darkness there was that familiar still small voice of hope within the pain that kept me looking forward for the turn. That voice kept me searching for the bend in the road that might reveal a spot of open air or ray of sunshine somewhere off in the distance. It spurred me on and kept me from drowning in self-pity. Isn't it funny how depression and hope often flow together down the same river?

God is speaking to my heart to give me a new, expanded vision for my future. He is showing me glimpses of what it might look like to pivot in a new, unfamiliar direction—one that is part ministry, part business, and part solitude and silence. My energies are being redirected, redefined. As I write this, I am realizing that the grief and emptiness of the past few months are being filled and transformed with the knowledge that God is with me in this transitional time and that it is He, not anything else, who will fill this and every future void in my life. He is indeed the Lifter of my head.

> *Why am I discouraged?*
> *Why is my heart so sad?*
> *I will put my hope in God!*
> *I will praise him again—*
> *my Savior and my God!*
>
> —*Psalm 42:11*